CAMILLE SAINT-SAËNS

CAMILLE SAINT-SAËNS

This is believed to be the last studio photograph, taken in
1921, before the death of the master.

ÇAMILLE SAINT-SAËNS

HIS LIFE AND ART

BY

WATSON LYLE

WITH A PREFACE BY
LEFF POUISHNOFF

ILLUSTRATED WITH A PORTRAIT OF CAMILLE
SAINT-SAËNS, AND MUSICAL ILLUSTRATIONS IN THE TEXT

GREENWOOD PRESS, PUBLISHERS
WESTPORT, CONNECTICUT

Originally published in 1923
by Kegan Paul, Trench, Trubner & Co., Ltd., London
and E.P. Dutton & Co., New York

First Greenwood Reprinting 1970

Library of Congress Catalogue Card Number 71-109776

SBN 8371-4266-0

Printed in the United States of America

I dedicate this book to the memory of my parents, who, from early childhood, guided and encouraged my love of music; and to whom, therefore, I largely owe the unfailing joy, and solace, which music brings to me.

WATSON LYLE.

The White House,
Navestock,
'Essex.

PREFACE

Every time the world loses one of its great ones, we instinctively feel the desire to turn our thoughts back in order to recall to our minds the principal events of his life. We are thus enabled to form our conclusions and find his rightful place in history.

All musicians, professional or amateur—all music-lovers, in fact — will welcome this opportune book on the life of that great musician, so extraordinarily gifted with the talents of composer, pianist, and organist— CAMILLE SAINT-SAENS.

I have not the slightest doubt that this work of Mr. WATSON LYLE'S will meet with a great success. The reader may see for himself with what love and care the author has carried out his task. He will be interested in the series of events from the musician's life chosen by the author and impressed by his logical sequence and convincing way of grouping them. He will likewise understand that only a true musician could give such a clear-sighted analysis of the composer's works, and will be duly grateful to the author on this account also.

For my part I congratulate Mr. Watson Lyle most sincerely on his book and wish him the great success which he deserves.

LEFF POUISHNOFF.

AUTHOR'S NOTE

I gratefully acknowledge the information kindly given me, towards the writing of this book, by the following friends :—Mme. Amina Goodwin, MM. H. A. Dean, Felix Goodwin, Arthur de Greef, Richard Hammond, Robert Moor, Leff Pouishnoff, H. Thompson, William L. Tilbrook, and Messrs. J. and W. Chester.

MM. A. Durand and Fils, Paris, have courteously authorised me to give the musical quotations.

WATSON LYLE.

CONTENTS

PART I

THE GROWTH OF A GENIUS

The records of the lives of the musically great impress one with the fact that the musician of exceptional merit, the master whose pre-eminence and genius is revealed by originality of achievement in his art, has usually given unmistakable evidence of his powers in early childhood.

But conversely, prodigies do not invariably develop into masters, or even into artists of outstanding merit. Too often the flame of genius in early life burns, and is encouraged to burn, with a fierceness that consumes the forces of supply at their source, and drains the reserve.

One can only feel anger with the elder Mozart at the manner in which he exploited the heaven-born talent of his son. Judiciously tended and cared for in early years, it is reasonable to assume that the pathetically brief life of the master might have run a longer, and even more important, course than it did.

Commencing to write this book upon Charles

Camille Saint-Saëns, one involuntarily reflects upon the signs of the possession of great musical gifts which the Austrian and French masters showed at a similarly tender age. Yet, had the physical and artistic growth of the French child been attended to in haphazard fashion there can be little doubt that posterity would not have heard of him; and that the art of music, and the development of it would have been poorer to the extent of his ceaseless productivity during close upon seventy of the full eighty-six years of his life.

Civilisation, in the formation and progress of which musical art has been, and is, an important factor, is under a debt to the memory of Mme. Saint-Saëns and of her aunt, Mme. Masson, for the wise and unremitting care which they devoted to the delicate infancy of the composer : and to the extreme care with which they helped, but avoided forcing, the inflorescence of his genius.

The fragile baby, born at No. 3, Rue du Jardinet, Paris, on the 9th October, 1835, certainly embarked upon his long life here under a severe handicap. Saint-Saëns, père, with the scourge of consumption already well advanced in his system at the time of his son's birth, died a couple of months later, on December 31st, just a year after his marriage. Medical opinion favoured the view that the germs of the disease had been communicated to the child.

Regarding his ancestry, Saint-Saëns has written that "this relationship (*i.e.*, with his maternal grand aunt) makes me a descendant of General Delcambre, one of the heroes of the retreat from Russia." And further, "My grand aunt was a precocious child—she walked at nine months—and she became a woman of keen intellect and brilliant attainments."

Mme. Masson adopted her niece, Clemence Collin, who in due course married M. Saint-Saëns, "a minor official in the Department of the Interior."

After the loss of her husband the young mother returned to the protection of her aunt, now also widowed, and on the advice of the doctors the infant Camille was left in the country with his nurse, at Corbeil.

The baby of two years who was brought back to the two women in Paris had become comparatively robust, and they, whom in after-life the master alluded affectionately to as his "two mothers" devoted themselves whole-heartedly to his growth, physically, intellectually and psychically.

His early environment was thus most congenial for his artistic growth; and the fine fruition to which his career attained is eloquent proof against the generally promulgated theory that genius often thrives best under hardship.

Both Saint-Saëns and Mozart possessed an unfailing and attractive melodic inspiration, a

facile technique, and a subtle appreciation of tone colour, although their sense of melody and colour differed. But the brief life of Mozart was one of grinding poverty, while up to the time of his death Saint-Saëns had little cause for monetary worry. These material circumstances give interest to the differing personalities expressed in their works; but they do not wholly explain it.

By outward indications of natural endowments, these two composers began life upon a fairly equal footing. But the difference in soul, personality, call it what you will, points to the existence of elements other than natural endowments and material circumstances in the evolution of genius—elements that are possibly born of emotional experiences which thus find an outlet and are reflected in the creative work of the artist.

The loving care, tempered by sound common sense of the two women upon whom, by natural circumstance, devolved the care of this genius in embryo, is surely reflected in the warm humanity of his music, and in the clearness of thought and adaptability to the opportunities of life that contributed largely towards the eminence of his professional career.

The little child of two and a half years old seated at the piano, pressing down the keys one by one and obviously experiencing great pleasure in listening to the gradual evaporation

of each sound, to the formation of the upper-partials thus created, before depressing the next key that, in its turn held the "Open, Sesame ! " to new wonders, was not admonished to cease trifling with the piano. He was not ordered to concentrate upon the cabalistic meaning of E.G.B.D.F. and F.A.C.E. He has recorded that the tales of the whippings and force used to make him learn his notes are sheer rubbish. The truth is that his great aunt, who undertook his preliminary musical education, gave the lessons a live interest for the little student by showing him the identical relation-ship of these mysterious signs with the sounds which he could create for himself and which he loved so well.

Thus early, then, was born and nourished the sensitive feeling for tone colour that distin-guishes the art of Saint-Saëns.

His innate sense of absolute pitch was shown when he correctly named, from an adjacent room, the sounds evoked by the tuner when tuning the piano. That was indeed a great game; almost as good fun as the gradual *crescendo* of hissing noises emitted by the big kettle "which was hung before the fire in the drawing-room every morning."

The "Method" (*i.e.*, instruction book) used by Mme. Masson was Le Carpentier's, and the eager child romped through it in a month. Such rapid progress betokened dangerous

B

activity of the young brain, and the piano was closed and the lessons suspended; but, as he himself tells us in his delightful " Ecole Buissonière," he " cried like a lost soul," and his aunt resumed the lessons.

His theoretical and practical knowledge advanced so rapidly that his initial attempts at composition began at the age of four; and when little over four and a half he excited much interest by his performance of the piano part in a Beethoven sonata for violin and pianoforte before a semi-private audience in the drawing-room of friends of his mother and aunt.

At that time he was frequently taken to the house on the Quai Voltaire where the painter Ingres lived with his wife.   Perhaps in this early friendship may be traced the dawning of ambitions and ideas of future greatness, for the painter talked to the child of Mozart, Gluck, Beethoven, and other great masters of music; and in his hero-worship the child of six dedicated an *Adagio* (how grave is youth!) of his own to the man.   Ingres, to show his appreciation of the compliment, gave his little friend a small medallion portrait of Mozart, with an inscription on the reverse side, " To M. Saint-Saëns, the charming interpreter of the divine artist."   Saint-Saëns, at that age, played Mozart's simpler piano sonatas exceedingly well.

In regard to the executive powers of the child

it is worthy of record that the drawing-room concert alluded to evidently revealed a young artist of such promise that the "*Moniteur Universel*" of 1.8.1840 gave the circumstance publicity.

Stamaty, a brilliant disciple of Kalkbrenner, undertook the continuance of his pianistic tuition at the age of seven, and he expressed his satisfaction at the soundness and completeness of Mme. Masson's teaching. There was, he said, nothing to do but perfect it.

The teacher of composition at Stamaty's school was a certain M. Maleden, who had perfected a wonderful system of harmony invented by Gottfried Weber, with whom he had studied in Germany. Maleden and his young pupil, Saint-Saëns, sometimes had heated discussions upon certain explanations that seemed obscure to the alert intelligence of the boy. The teacher, a kind and somewhat timid soul, would hold the boy's head down close to the table in an endeavour to force him into a promise of blind obedience. But as the refractory youth stuck to his own opinions, and refused to alter them by brute force, the master was generally driven into a compromise. Soon after he commenced his studies with Maleden, the boy, anxious to experiment with this addition to his knowledge of music, began serious composition. His creative bent turned into the direction of a pianoforte sonata; and overtures, cantatas, and

songs were also written, none of which the artist of maturity allowed to be published.

He was already becoming known in the *salons* of fashionable Paris, in the half-patronising, half-wondering manner in which clever children attract attention in artistic and quasi-artistic circles the world over. At the house of Ingres he met Delsarte, who ruined his own voice and those whom he "trained"; and Henri Reber, whom in maturity he was to succeed at the Institute. His musical pabulum at this time consisted chiefly of the works of J. S. Bach, Beethoven, and Mozart, with a leavening of pianoforte composers of the day, such as Kalkbrenner.

Other executive artists have made their official débuts as pianists at an earlier age than Saint-Saëns did, and have sustained careers of undiminished brilliance—Carreño, for instance, first appeared at the age of nine and was a distinguished artist for the remaining fifty years of her life—but I cannot recollect any who have appeared as prodigies during the lifetime of the great Frenchman and who developed to the same extent as he did.

Stamaty decided that he was sufficiently advanced to be definitely launched upon his professional career, and a concert was arranged for him in the Sallé Pleyel, Paris, on May 6th, 1846. He was, therefore, ten years and seven months old when he made his début.

An Italian orchestra, conducted by Tilmant, was engaged for the occasion. The young artist played the parts for solo pianoforte in Beethoven's Concerto No. 3 in C minor and in a Mozart Concerto in B flat. He also played some smaller pieces, a Sonata of Hummel, a Prélude and Fugue of Bach, and items of Handel and Kalkbrenner. All these he played from memory, which was not only very unusual at that time, but, even many years later, was an innovation that was frowned upon by the hidebound pedants. This concert was a tremendous success, and the boy was hailed by the press of the day as a second Mozart.

Stamaty (teachers then and now appear to have been very similar!) was keen to exploit his amazingly talented pupil, and there was some talk of a performance at the Société des Concerts du Conservatoire. Seghers, who afterwards proved such a good friend to the boy, objected because he detested Stamaty; and he was a power in the conduct of the orchestra. However, the teacher persisted in his attempts in induce Mme. Saint-Saëns to allow her son to appear at more concerts, but she, deciding that the fleeting success of a hardly-worked prodigy should not be allowed to endanger the triumph of the matured artist, declined to consider the matter, and a coolness resulted which ended the tutorship. A friend remonstrated with Mme. Saint-Saëns for allowing her boy to

play Beethoven Sonatas, then considered food
for grown-ups only.   In reply to the sarcastic
enquiry as to what music her son would play
when he was twenty she made the strangely-
prophetic reply that he would play his own.
Saint-Saëns has related the incident at length
in his "École Buissonière."

During the half-dozen years that followed,
his attention, excepting for a few public appearances, was directed to his further education,
musical and general.   At the age of fourteen
Stamaty introduced him to Benoist, at the
Conservatoire, and the boy was seated at the
keyboard of the organ to see what he could do.
But he was so frightened at the strange sounds
elicited that the class laughed, and Benoist only
agreed to accept him as a listening pupil for
organ.

He "listened" during classes to considerable purpose, and also worked hard at home
studying the "Forty-eight" of Bach, and one
day, when all the chosen pupils failed at the
instrument, Benoist bethought him of his
"ugly duckling" and ordered the child to play.
This he did, to the utmost satisfaction of the
teacher, who then accepted him as a regular
pupil.   That year he won the second prize, and
but for his youth would have been awarded the
first.   Benoist, who was an excellent teacher,
but a quite ordinary player, paid more attention to the youth after that, and frequently

chatted with, and encouraged, him, apart from his regular lessons.

Maleden fortunately completed the instruction of his pupil in harmony, counterpoint, and fugue. One writes " fortunately " advisedly, because Halévy, under whose care he passed at the age of fifteen for composition, while a student at the Conservatoire, discharged his responsibilities as a teacher in a most haphazard fashion. Frequently Halévy would not turn up, and usually he was deeply engrossed, at classes, in composing opera and opéra-comique of the made-to-order brand that nevei survived more than a few performances. He was a kind-hearted, and evidently weak-willed, soul, and gave audiences to all manner of possible and impossible singers who called to see him at the Conservatoire about engagements in his productions. In his absence the young genius would betake himself to the library and there devour the scores of ancient and contemporary composers with all the enthusiasm of early youth. Had he not been already well grounded in the fundamental technique of composition this negligence of Halévy might, of course, have proved very detrimental to his progress. As it was, the score reading helped his ideas of orchestration as much, probably, as reams of paper work could have done.

Compositions of various kinds were sketched out or completed during the years at the

Conservatoire, but the faculty of self-criticism engendered by his common-sense training decreed the consignment of the majority of these early works to oblivion. An idea of the correctness of his estimate of his own early work may be gained from the fact that his first entry for the Prix de Rome in 1852 was unsuccessful. However, later in that year, he won a prize for composition offered by the Société de Saint Cécile, recently inaugurated by Seghers, with an "Ode" to the Saint.

Two years previously, when Saint-Saëns was fifteen, Seghers planned a series of concerts at which the boy was to appear as solo-pianist. But the project had to be abandoned because of the uncurable nervousness of Seghers whenever he attempted to play, as a violinist, in public. Apparently, too, he belonged to that unfortunate section of humanity whose enthusiasm for a new idea far exceeds their tenacity of purpose in putting it into practice.

In December, 1852, Saint-Saëns was appointed to his first professional post. This engagement, as organist in the Church of Saint Méry, he held for five years.

The following year his symphony in E flat, not published until 1855, was produced by the Société de Saint Cécile, anonymously, under Seghers. Prejudices against the performance of works by unknown composers (as if everybody has not been, at one time "unknown"!)

was even greater then than now, and Seghers knew very well that if the symphony was put before the committee as signed by his young friend it would be contemptuously tossed aside. He therefore said that it had been sent to him, anonymously, from Germany.

The symphony was enthusiastically praised. At the rehearsal the youth of eighteen, all trembling for the success of this year-old child of his brain, listened to a conversation regarding it between Berlioz and Gounod, who were already interested in him, but were unaware that he was the author of the work they had just heard. They freely discussed the good and bad points of the composition and were naturally greatly astonished when they learnt, after the public performance, that the young man, whose ideas they had sought to improve by their discussion of the new symphony, was actually its composer.

This work may be regarded as signalising the beginning of the master's career as a composer. It will be considered in detail later, with its numerous and varied successors. We are mainly concerned here with the influences and affairs of private life that may be regarded as having helped to shape the art and life of Saint-Saëns.

This incident of the rehearsal went towards the cementing of his friendship with Berlioz and Gounod, both of whom took a very real and

helpful interest in his early life. At that time
Gounod wrote him a short, but noble, letter of
congratulation upon his success. He pointed
out the moral responsibility that his natural endowments placed him under to become a "great
master" and adjured him to persevere. The
letter was treasured by its recipient throughout
his life.

Saint-Saëns' sympathetic insight into human
nature probed beneath the outward crust of
moroseness and arrogance which Berlioz presented to society in general. His own disposition, optimistic and sunny, even to the extent
of frivolity, was so utterly different from that of
the forbidding Hector that, by the law of the
attraction of opposites, one can readily compre-
hend the affectionate regard in which he held
Berlioz.

Gounod understood pretty clearly the composition of Saint-Saëns' psychical make-up;
and he had a well-balanced appreciation of the
the strong and weak points in his technical
armoury.

He recognised the chameleon-like adaptability that was at once a strength and a danger
to the young composer. A strength, because
of the ability to absorb impressions of "local
colour" and exotic idioms which it gave him,
along with a complete understanding of the art
of his contemporaries, Rossini, Verdi, Schumann, Mendelssohn, and Wagner, to mention

the barest few who were in the van. And a
danger, in case it should prevent originality of
expression and cause him to degenerate into a
mere imitator.   When Gounod said of him,
"He writes as he feels, and with what he
knows," he demonstrated his perfect compre-
hension of the character and methods of
Saint-Saëns.

A visit to Rome with the Abbé Gabriel, curé
of the Church of Saint Méry, enabled the composer to hear the famous singers of the Sistine
Chapel. But there is no record as to whether he
attempted to write out from memory the music
which he had heard, and which is so zealously
guarded against access by the casual visitor;
and thus to emulate the famous achievement of
Mozart, who, after a similar visit in 1770, wrote
out the whole of the *Misérère* of Allegri, which
is composed for two choirs of nine voices.
The abbé took his young organist to Rome as
a sign of his appreciation of the Mass that
Saint-Saëns had dedicated to him.

The youth, maturing to manhood, was no
moody recluse. Fond of gaiety and change,
he found congenial relaxation from his studies
and from composing and his profession as an
executant, in the by no means heavy musical
fare provided at the Opéra-Comique.

His mother held Monday evening receptions
at her flat in Paris, and at these he was often the
personification of fun and high spirits.   On

these occasions music was, quite inevitably, the paramount attraction; and it is evident that these reunions provided opportunities for meeting personalities likely to be interested in Saint-Saëns and likely to be of importance in his career.

The young artist and his friends frequently arranged operatic performances, in costume, for the receptions, to the entertainment of the guests. Saint-Saëns often assumed the rôle of a female character, a type of impersonation for which his high-pitched voice particularly suited him.

The *salons* of Mme. Viardot, a friend of Mme. Saint-Saëns, a sister of Mme. Malibran, and, of course, famous as a singer and teacher of singing in her day, were also the scene of these revels, as well as the rendezvous for chamber music performances and recitals of a private kind by the singer and her friends. On one of these evenings at Mme. Viardot's Saint-Saëns appeared in a burlesque of Gounod's " Faust " as Marguerite, discovering the jewels and mirror in the casket, and warbling the florid music of the heroine! At Mme. Viardot's he listened to a performance, by his hostess and Clara Schumann, of a duet Sonata by Schumann.

He was a frequent visitor to the home of the Seghers, and it was there, one memorable day, at the age of eighteen, that he first met Liszt.

The great pianist had been so long absent from Paris that his reappearance was in the nature of a resurrection. His personality and playing made a profound impression upon Saint-Saëns, and he included the young Frenchman in his circle of protégés of art— this great, good, and generous-minded artist to whose help and encouragement so many young musicians of that and the previous decade owed recognition and success.

M. and Mme. Viardot took Saint-Saëns to one of Rossini's famous "evenings" in his splendid apartment at the corner of the Chausée d'Antin.   Saint-Saëns was received by the distinguished Italian composer with the superficial cordiality that he extended towards those who were brought to him, possibly as pianists or composers desiring his social and artistic patronage.   After the production of "Guillaume Tell," Rossini rested upon his laurels, and in a social way, in Paris, basked in the after-glow of his earlier triumphs in art. To be a frequenter of his *soirées* gave a cachet of distinction to the professional reputation of young artists; and it must be admitted that, as in the case of many another such "court" both before and since, the courtiers consisted largely of flatterers and parasites upon art, all of whom, however, Rossini appears to have valued at their true worth.

When he learnt that his young visitor could

most certainly not be placed in the category of any of these self-seekers, and was undoubtedly an artist of promise, he altered his attitude of patronage and invited his guest to pay him a morning call.

Rossini, on more intimate acquaintance, proved to be very different from Rossini the courted and flattered. His ideas upon musical art of the day were at least broad and noble, if they were a little out of date. Saint-Saëns became a frequent visitor at his house and often played or acted as accompanist at the evening receptions at the *appartement* in the Chausée d'Antin.

The first performance of the Tarantelle (Op. 6) for flute and clarinet was arranged for one of these receptions by Rossini, to take place under circumstances of anonymity that recall the initial performance of the Symphony in E flat of the young composer.

Two noted artists of the day, Dorus and Leroy, readily agreed to play the duet, and as there was no written programme the guests were under the impression that the new work was from the pen of their host.

At the conclusion of the *soirée musicale* the flatterers and fawning admirers pressed their congratulations upon Rossini, acclaiming the composition as a masterpiece. The elderly musician allowed the practical joke to run to its uttermost limits in this way, and then, taking

hold of his protégé's hand, announced the authorship of the duet and quietly "floored" the sycophants.

The incident was worthy of the mood which prompted Saint-Saëns to write a one-act parody, "Gabriella di Vergy," upon the old-style Italian opera, for performance by himself and his friends at one of his mother's "Monday" receptions.

When one remembers that during these years (1852-8) he wrote, in addition to the works particularly mentioned, another symphony, which, with its immediate successor in that form, remains unpublished, concertos for pianoforte, and for violin, and orchestra, the Messe Solenelle, about which Liszt wrote to him so encouragingly (on 19.7.1869), besides many smaller pieces, one realises that indulgence in relaxation did not lead to any slackening of his energies professionally.

The next position as organist which he filled was at the Church of the Madeleine. He commenced an engagement there, in 1858, that lasted nineteen years, and afforded him a yearly remuneration of f.3,000.

In addition to the material certainty which this appointment carried, it was an exceedingly helpful one, because of the professional status and social opportunities connected with it, and that rendered the post a fortunate one from every point of view. His immediate predeces-

sor was Lefébure Wély, famed as an improviser more than as a composer; and his successors were Théodore Dubois and Gabriel Fauré, both of whom became distinguished in musical art.

Saint-Saëns was appointed to a professorship at the École Niedermeyer in 1860, but relinquished his duties there in 1863. Fauré was a pupil of his during that time, and so also was André Messager.

He had often seen Richard Wagner during his constant attendances, as a child, at the Société des Concerts. Wagner was then a young man, and he also went to the Société frequently. But the famous meeting between the two composers did not occur until 1861, at the Opéra, when the ability of the young Frenchman-to play at sight, on the pianoforte, from complicated full scores in MS. amazed the German. The occasion was the production of "Tannhaüser" in Paris. Later, at Bayreuth, Wagner is reported to have toasted Saint-Saëns as the greatest living French composer. In fact, he was apparently much more impressed by the personality of the Frenchman than that individual was by his.

A holiday in the Pyrenees in 1863 was evidently responsible for the inspiration, and much of the atmosphere, of the Trio in F composed in that year.

The tone colour of this Trio bears early evi-

dence of the composer's extreme sensitiveness to his surroundings.   He was especially susceptible to the influence of Nature.   One finds ample signs of this in his later works.

The Fantaisie, "Africa" (written in Cairo) and the Fifth Pianoforte Concerto, in F, also conceived during one of his many visits to Egypt, are two outstanding examples of the effects of extraneous suggestion upon his creative genius.

In 1864 he again tried, unsuccessfully, to win the Prix de Rome.   Academic honours undeniably possess a value in their assessment of technical knowledge; but this incident, relating to the early career of an artist whose art has attained international distinction, serves to emphasise the fact that success in competition is not necessarily any criterion of artistic worth.

Between Bizet, who with Delibes was a fellow-student at the Conservatoire, and Saint-Saëns existed a very sincere and intimate friendship; and Bizet had won the Prix de Rome in 1857.

The two young composers were almost of an age—to be exact Bizet was the junior by three years—and had sympathetic interests.   But the theatre was Bizet's congenial environment. The reputation of his brief career rests there; and it reached its culmination in "Carmen," produced at the Opera in the year of his death, 1875.

C

About the period under consideration
(1863-4) Bizet's opera "Les Pécheurs des
Perles" had achieved its début. Rather naturally, then, Saint-Saëns' ideas floated opera-
wards, and he sketched out the music for the
five acts of "Le Timbre d'Argent" in two
months. But the opera underwent many
changes and received many checks against
production before it finally appeared as his
second work in this form given publicly. The
Franco-German War and the fall of the Second
Empire was, perhaps, Fate's unkindest cut,
when at length details of production seemed to
be in a fair way of running smoothly.

A triumph, of a quasi-academic nature,
occurred to him at the competition arranged by
the Imperial Government at the International
Exhibition of 1867. His cantata, "Les Noces
de Prométhèe," was adjudged the winner over
100 other entries. Amongst the judges was
Berlioz, who was naturally most elated at the
success of his young friend.

Rubinstein, who five years earlier had
founded the Conservatoire of Music in Petro-
grad (St. Petersburg then), relinquished his
position of director there and came to Paris.
He planned a series of concerts, at which he
invited Saint-Saëns, whom he had previously
met, to officiate as conductor.

Eventually, at the ninth concert of the series,
Saint-Saëns appeared as soloist in the first per-

formance of his own Pianoforte Concerto in
G minor (No. 2, Op. 22), which he had roughly
written out in three weeks' time.   The performance, according to his own account, was
a somewhat ragged one, perhaps owing to the
phenomenal rapidity with which the work had
been composed.   However, the occasion also
served as the first appearance in Paris, as conductor, of the composer's friend, Rubinstein;
and the Scherzo, at least, of the new concerto
captivated the enthusiasm of the audience.

One finds here another instance of the sound
reasoning and adaptability to circumstances
which frequently helped the onward course of
the artist.

In the desire which Rubinstein expressed to
conduct a concert in Paris the opportunity presented itself to the composer of securing an
auspicious premiérè for a new work of his own
—the concerto—which was already taking shape
in his brain, and he worked energetically to
complete it in the short time at his disposal.

The spontaneity and freshness of the music,
apart from the evergreen popularity of the
work with concert-givers thereafter, is against
all theory of it having been a " pot-boiling "
effort.

This series of concerts was the means of
cementing a delightful friendship between the
two men, both already famous in the same
branches of their art.   They also helped to

direct public and official attention more insistently to the dawning greatness of the young Frenchman. The seal of official recognition took the form of the Decoration of the Légion d'Honneur.

Anxious for the opinion of Liszt, Saint-Saëns sent a parcel containing some of his works to the master for criticism. Idealism, vivifying as the light and warmth of the sun, irradiated the relationship of Liszt with his fellow-artists and enabled him to give them advice that was helpful because of its complete freedom from thoughts of self.

In a letter dated July 19th, 1869, he expressed his warm appreciation, and helpfully commented upon the Messe Solennelle (Op. 4), composed in 1856; and although his own Mass had been but recently produced, his reply to Saint-Saëns was absolutely free from petty ideas of rivalry. For Liszt such things simply did not exist.

His friendship had about it none of the transitory characteristics of acquaintanceship. Ten years later, for example, he was instrumental in securing the initial performance of "Samson et Dalila" (then called simply "Dalila") at Weimar.

As an outward indication of the admiration which Saint-Saëns felt for Liszt his attempts at the further exploration of the art-form, the Symphonic Poem, which Liszt created, bears evidence.

During the awful days that began with the surrounding of Paris by the Germans, on Sept. 19th, 1870, Saint-Saëns endured much, mentally and physically. Until the terrors of the Commune, in the following March, he became a soldier of the National Guard. The loss, at Buzenal, of his friend Henri Regnault, the painter, of whom he was very fond, was a personal bereavement of the siege. He composed his " Marche Heroïque" and dedicated it to the memory of Regnault.

Regnault was not only a painter of distinction but possessed a fine tenor voice, and had received a musical education at the Conservatoire. He was able, therefore, to take a living interest in the art of his friend, and he was the first interpreter of " Les Mélodies Persanes,'" composed at the beginning of the war. Saint-Saëns dedicated " Sabre en main" to him.

The friends saw each other for the last time a few days before Buzenal. Regnault, rifle in hand, was starting out for drill practice. He stopped before his easel on which rested an unfinished water colour. At the bottom of the painting was a shapeless mass of colour. By means of his handkerchief, moistened by saliva, he feverishly worked away at this spot with his disengaged hand, and finally there emerged from it the head of a lion, considerably to the awe of Saint-Saëns, who stood by.

Another loss sustained by the composer from

amongst his friends was that of the Abbé Deguerry, to whose good offices he was largely indebted for his appointment at the Madeleine. The priest was one of the hostages shot by the Communists.

A reflection of these days exists in the deep emotion and anguish that pervades the Sonata in C minor (No. 1, Op. 32) for violoncello and pianoforte, conceived as an outcome of the experiences undergone by the composer.

The red days of horror that during March 18th to May 29th razed the Tuileries, Hôtel de Ville, and Palais Royal sent Saint-Saëns with other refugees to London, and but for the Commune it is quite probable that the long acquaintance of the master with England, begun then, would have been considerably delayed.

The necessity for his sudden departure interrupted the activities of the new Société Nationale de Musique, which, with M. Romain Bussine, professor of singing at the Conservatoire, he had just formed.

Gounod was also amongst the distinguished refugees who found sanctuary in the English capital, and the two friends of course met.

The distinction of introducing Saint-Saëns to the musical life of the Metropolis, and incidentally of England, belongs to John Ella, under whom, at one of the concerts of the Musical Union, he appeared in London.

The master returned to his own country upon the suppression of the Commune, and entered immediately on a period of great activity, creatively and in concert work.

He renewed his efforts to get "Le Timbre d'Argent" produced, this time at the Opéra-Comique. The then manager, M. Camille du Locle, suggested that while they awaited the return of better days, Saint-Saëns should write a one-act work. He proposed a collaboration with Louis Gallet, a stranger to Saint-Saëns, but of whom du Locle said, "You were made to understand each other."

He judged aright. The two were duly introduced and the friendship of the collaborators proceeded apace, and lasted from that time, 1871, until the death of Gallet from a painful disease, in 1899. In his "Ecole Buissonière" the composer has thrown considerable light upon that happy collaboration. He alludes to Gallet as "the diligent and chosen companion of my best years, whose support was so dear and precious to me," and : "Outside our work, too, the relationship was delightful. We wrote to each other constantly in both prose and verse; we bombarded each other with sonnets. His letters were sometimes ornamented with water colours, for he drew very well, and one of his joys was to cover white paper with colour."

Oddly enough, Gallet was not Saint-Saëns' collaborator in the opera that has brought him

most fame, " Samson et Dalila." That work was really begun in 1870, before he knew Gallet, to a libretto of Ferdinand Lemaire. The first fruits of the collaboration was the one-act opera, " La Princesse Jaune," which marked the operatic début of Saint-Saëns at the Opéra-Comique on June 12th, 1872. It met with only a lukewarm reception, but was revived in later years.

On July 30th, 1874, Saint-Saëns made the first of his appearances at the concerts of the Royal Philharmonic Society in London. On that occasion he played the part for solo instrument in Beethoven's Concerto in G for pianoforte and orchestra, although he had hoped to present one of the three concertos for the pianoforte which he had already written. The directors, at that time, decided upon the Beethoven work. The other soloists were Mlle. Tietjens and Charles Santley.

In 1875 occurred the death of Bizet. The psychical effect of this loss may perhaps be traced in the mood of questioning with which the Fourth Pianoforte Concerto opens, and in the Chorale of the Quartet in B flat, Op. 41.

Victor Hugo was among those who returned to Paris after the fall of the Second Empire, and in due course Saint-Saëns, who had idealised the man from reading his poems, years before, met the hero of his imagination. Contrary to his preconceived idea of the per-

sonality of Liszt, which fell far short of the reality when met, the illustrious author made a quite ordinary impression. His reception of the young composer was hearty enough. He came forward to Saint-Saëns, when he was presented, both hands outstretched in greeting and expressions of pleasure upon his lips.

However, there was a fascination about Hugo which encouraged the artist to go to his evening receptions as often as possible, to listen to his polished phraseology and engaging conversation. The intimacy suffered an interruption that lasted for some years. The poet insinuated that he would be pleased if Saint-Saëns would set to music *La Esmeralda*. The musician in the composer warned him of the impossibility of accomplishing the work creditably, and he affected not to see the hint given by his host; but he did not go near Hugo's house for a long time after that.

Throughout the latter half of his life, work, and still more work, was the narcotic he favoured to heal the wounds that Fate meted out to his affectionate nature.

In May, 1878, a grief of the most poignant description occurred to him. His eldest son, a baby of two and a half years old, fell from a fourth floor window and was killed. The sinister chain of coincidence which often shows in the occurrence of a second or third death in a family circle within a short space of time

proved its existence in the case of Saint-Saëns by robbing him, soon after, of his second son, an infant only seven months old.

Even now, one shrinks from meditating upon the acute agony that the doubly-bereaved father must have suffered.

Although his engagement at the Madeleine had terminated during the previous year, and he was free to that extent to leave Paris and seek forgetfulness in foreign travel, he chose instead the panacea of work, and devoted himself to the completion of his third opera, "Étienne Marcel."

Imagine, then, the tremendous strength of will and powers of concentration that made the creation of music to fit the action of the opera possible under the private circumstances of the composer's life. Gaiety, as much as tragedy, called for musical expression. The work cannot be regarded as representative of its creator at his highest level; but the failing is more one of superficiality, a kind of mechanical emotionalism, than of technique or sterility of idea. At the same time one must remember that the opera was a commissioned one, both Gallet and Saint-Saëns having availed themselves of an opportunity that presented itself when Aimè Gros, a friend of the composer, who had lately taken over the management of the Grand Theatre at Lyons, asked him for a work.

In the summer of 1879 he attended the

Birmingham Musical Festival for the production of his cantata "The Lyre and the Harp."

The opinion which he afterwards expressed, publicly, in favour of the English as a thoroughly musical nation is doubly interesting. His criticism of the choristers at the Festival reads :—

"Accuracy, precision in time and rhythm, finesse in the lights and shades, charm in the sonority—this wonderful chorus unites everything. If people who sing like this are not musicians, they do exactly what they would do if they were the best musicians in the world."

Considerable courage was necessary in 1879 to make this assertion; and that Saint-Saëns should have done it is eloquent of his sturdy independence of thought, and his steady refusal to accept "made opinions" on any subject. Investigation came more naturally to him, from the days of babyhood when love of exploration manifested itself in the thoughtful depression of the keys of the pianoforte. Thus, indeed, was the child father of the man.

The soundness of the dictum which Saint-Saëns formulated on that remote occasion is borne out to-day by the prominent position which Britain occupies in the musical art of the world.

The composer maintained his devotion to his art with unabated vigour, appearing in the triple rôle of solo pianist, conductor, and composer

on the Continent. He also became friendly with the librarian at Buckingham Palace, and was allowed access to the music MSS. there.

In a bundle of harpsichord music of the Sixteenth Century he found a theme which he used ultimately as the basis of his opera, "Henry VIII.," and in the "Coronation March" (Op. 117, written in 1902 for King Edward VII.).

It is probable that the idea of the opera alluded to occurred during the examination of these old MSS. at Buckingham Palace; at any rate, he began to compose the music for it about that time. He was also elected a member of the Institute when Henri Reber died. Reber was a composer whose chamber music was popular during the youth of Saint-Saëns.

This period (about 1881) also included the *rapprochement* with Victor Hugo, to which the "Hymne à Victor Hugo" was a contributory factor.

In connection with the erection of a statue to the poet, celebrations were planned, including an important one at the Trocadéro. Memories stirred within the composer and he wrote the Hymne. Victor Hugo was somewhat chagrined at the rate at which the subscriptions for the statue came in; the response was not overwhelming enough to suit his ideas, so he had the subscription stopped, and Saint-Saëns regretfully put his composition away.

However, Bruneau père, the father of Alfred Bruneau, the composer, planned a series of spring concerts at the Trocadéro and went to Saint-Saëns for an unpublished work, and the Hymne came forth from its seclusion.

The whole thing was a tremendous success. The audience applauded the poet (who seldom made a public appearance) vociferously, and he, in turn, fêted and elated, extended the olive branch to his estranged friend, who took it eagerly. The friendship was thus resumed and lasted until the death of the poet in 1885.

The somewhat feverish existence, professional and private, upon which the composer had entered continued until the spring of 1883, when he learnt the lesson that the human machine, especially when it happens to be a highly specialised mechanism like his was, sooner or later reaches a condition that imperatively calls for rest to avoid the snapping of some vital part, weakened to breaking point, by the heat of the tension generated by long and high productivity.

Soon after the first performance of " Henry VIII.," on March 5th, 1883, therefore, he followed the advice of his doctor and sought rest and rejuvenation in sunny Algeria. He completed the cure at Cauterets before returning, in October, to his busy life in Paris. " Henry VIII." was announced at the Opéra, and " Étienne Marcel " at the Théâtre du Chateau d'Eau.

Liszt had given the first performance of
" Samson et Dalila " at Weimar, and its immediate success there was followed by others in
the chief centres of music in Germany. All
this helped in the consolidation of Saint-Saëns'
reputation as a composer of Opéra Grand.

Soon after the production of "Samson" he
used his influence to get a work of Massenet's,
who was a contemporary and a rival of that
period, performed at Weimar. He was therefore greatly hurt by the icy reception given
him in private by Massenet when he received
the news that his work had also been staged at
Weimar. Poor Saint-Saëns had, quite naturally, expected at least the show of friendship
which Massenet did not scruple to shower upon
him in public.

A request from the Royal Philharmonic
Society of London, for a new symphony,
arrived at an opportune time for the return of
the composer's physical health and vigour. His
response to the invitation took the form of the
Third Symphony in C minor, which was produced at a concert of the Society on May 19th,
1886, and in Paris on the 9th and 16th of the
January following by the orchestra of the
Société des Concerts.

The master himself conducted the London
performance, and he dedicated the work to
Liszt. The death of Liszt occurred, as we
know, in July of that year, and the inscription

on the published score therefore reads, "to the memory of Franz Liszt."

The exceptional powers, as a symphonist, revealed in this work, occasions regret, in the interests of the development of musical art, that Saint-Saëns did not expend more energy in the writing of symphonies and less upon opera, an art form which was not his most congenial expressive medium.

He left five symphonies and thirteen stage works (ominous number!). One cannot imagine a diminution—probably the reverse—in the total success of his artistic career had these proportions been more equal, or even made *vice-versa*. The explanation of the actual state of affairs may lie in the commonsense view, that although it is more difficult to secure the production of an opera than of a symphony, the opera, unless it absolutely fails, is likely to attain the greater number of performances right off. On the other hand, a symphony, with its one or two performances during the first month of its existence, as against the half-dozen performances of a moderately-successful opera before it is taken off, would involve very much less financial support.

In 1887 he made another notable appearance in London at a concert organised by the late Mr. Wilhelm Ganz, at which he played the part for solo pianoforte in his Fourth Concerto for that instrument and orchestra.

The cosmopolitan love of travel and change increased in Saint-Saëns with the passage of years. Early in 1890 he left Paris upon a journey to the Canaries. There he laid aside his art and enjoyed a delightful rest from the strain of public life. He adopted another name, and did not leave any address to which letters could be forwarded.

To this period of voluntary obscurity one of his literary works, the "Rimes Familières," probably belongs.

The rest, physical, emotional and mental, which he sought was ended, after a few delightful months *incognito*, by his recognition in Las Palmas. When once his identity was noised abroad peace was at an end for the recluse. He said, pathetically, that crowds of well-intentioned people invaded his life and rendered it unendurable. The lot of a celebrity in a city is bad enough, but the lot of a celebrity in a small town is robbed of all privacy. And as life in Paris presented greater possibilities of seclusion then, than a continuance of life in Las Palmas, to Paris he returned : at least, for a time.

However, in the winter of 1891, he went to Ceylon, and on the journey home tarried at Cairo where the Fantasia, "Africa," for piano and orchestra, was composed. The work is one of the most popular of all he has written for that combination. It positively exhales the

heat-haze and brilliance of Egyptian days and the mysterious spirit of the sparkling starlight in the deep blue dome of clear, cold nights beside the Nile.

The Fantasia is an arresting example of the inherent ability of Saint-Saëns to translate the very atmosphere of his surroundings into terms of music; to transfigure his material circumstances, and his emotions, so that they are intuitively sensed in the imagination of his hearers.

Another visit to his native land was succeeded by a sojourn in Algiers. He wrote a comedy, " La Crampe des Écrivains " (one act), which was produced at the Municipal Theatre.

On New Year's Day, 1893, he appeared in London at a concert of the Philharmonic Society as soloist in his Concerto No. 2 in G minor for piano and orchestra, and also conducted the performance of his Symphonic Poem, " Le Rouet d'Omphale," while Tschaikowsky conducted his Fourth Symphony in F. The occasion was certainly unique in the London concert world.

Saint-Saëns was very delighted with the cordial reception given to him at Cambridge in the following June, and with the hospitality extended to him during his stay in that town. The Honorary Degree of Doctor of Music was conferred upon him then, and also upon Max Bruch, Tschaikowsky, Boïto, and Greig. The Norwegian master was unable to be present,

D

and of the others all, like him, ultimately pre-
deceased the French composer. He was the
soloist in a performance of his new Fantasia,
" Africa," which provided one of the items at
a concert arranged on that occasion.

Now almost as restless as any globe-trotter,
he next visited Saigong, in the Far East. The
spirit of exploration and discovery animated
him rather than the vulgar boastfulness that
urges your more mundane traveller to journey
chiefly because he likes to say " *I've* been there
—and there—and there—!"; and yet who
might as well remain at home, so seldom do his
excursions appear to extend far beyond the
surroundings of his hotel, in the countries
visited. The master regarded his travels as a
means of still further extending his knowledge
of the human race and of enriching his art by
the variety of his experiences.

He was composing all the time. Sometimes
new works of magnitude, sometimes altering
others that he considered unsatisfactory. In
one case (while in the East) completing the
score of an opera " Frédégonde," left unfinished by a friend of his old student days,
Ernest Guiraud, who had died. Memories of
the days when he, Bizet, Guiraud, and Delibes
were fellow-students and companions must
have crowded upon him as he worked at his
dutiful task, in surroundings differing vastly
from those conjured by memory.

Another performance of his Symphony No. 3 in C minor was given in London at the Philharmonic on June 7th, 1895, under his direction, with Mr. W. S. Hoyte at the organ and Mr. Henry Bird and Dr. Norman Cummings at the two pianofortes; and a Jubilee Concert was given in Paris the following year to celebrate the fiftieth anniversary of his official début into professional musical life at the Sallé Pleyel on May 6th, 1846.

M. Castlebon de Beauxhostes, an amateur musician of considerable wealth, conceived the idea of arranging open-air theatrical performances with music in some arenas at Beziers, in Southern France. The arenas were originally intended to accommodate bull-fighting exhibitions.

Saint-Saëns, ever versatile and adaptable in the employment of his musical gifts and knowledge, undertook to supply an important musical setting for a tragedy written by his friend, Louis Gallet, entitled " Déjanire." As a result of the project came the highly-successful performance at the production in August, 1898.

The composer was in command of the orchestra and a large chorus of male and female voices. The material of this production, musical and literary, it is worth remembering, formed the nucleus of the opera of the same name that was given at Monte Carlo almost thirteen years later (14.3.1911) and at the Opera, Paris, on 22.11.1911.

Gallet, seriously ill, in fact dying, journeyed to Beziers in 1899 for the second production of " Déjanire." His condition of exhaustion, which aggravated the deafness from which he suffered, made it impossible for him to hear anything, not even the plaudits of the thousands of spectators. He died soon afterwards.

In the winter after the première of " Déjanire," Saint-Saëns again visited the Canary Islands, and then proceeded to Buenos Aires to give a series of chamber concerts. Within a few months, however, he returned to Europe and appeared at concerts in Brussels with Ysaÿe, to whom the string quartet No. 1, Op. 112, is dedicated.

At the Paris Exhibition in May, 1900, his cantata, " Le Feu Céleste," was produced at the opening concert. The succeeding five years saw the birth of three new operas, and the incidental music to Mme. Jane Dieulafoy's " Parysatis," some numbers from which, such as the " Air du Rossignol," are frequently heard in concert halls here. For one of the operas alluded to, " Hélène," he was his own librettist. It was produced at Monte Carlo on February 18th, 1904, eleven months later at the Opéra-Comique, and afterwards at Covent Garden, with Melba in the title-rôle.

A trip to the United States, undertaken to keep engagements in Philadelphia, Chicago, and Washington, was physically an unpleasant

experience. He became very ill on the journey, and was really unwell until he proceeded to Cairo to recuperate. Despite all this, however, his capacity for finding variety and enjoyment in life and in his surroundings enabled him to derive considerable pleasure from the American tour. He was well received by the Americans, and his impressions of them were most agreeable. Gratitude for his recovery from the illness of this period found expression in a setting of " Praise ye the Lord."

Most celebrities have statues erected to their memory after death; but Saint-Saëns had the somewhat unique experience of being present at the unveiling of a statue of himself erected at Dieppe, where is also the Musée de Saint-Saëns, in 1907.

The veteran violoncellist, Joseph Hollman, gave a concert in Queen's Hall on June 7th, 1910, to celebrate the 25th anniversary of the first appearance in England of Saint-Saëns. The programme was devoted to the works of the composer, and was as follows :—Quartet for pianoforte, violin, viola, and violoncello (Op. 41), in which the artists were the composer, Ysaÿe, Hollander, and Hollman. This was followed by three songs, " La Cloche," " Le bonheur est chose legére," and "Aimons-nous," sung by Miss Esta d'Argo. These were succeeded by what was then a new work, " La Muse et le Poète," specially composed for the

occasion, said to have been suggested by de Musset's " La Nuit d'Octobre," and performed by Ysaÿe and Hollman, with the master in charge of the pianoforte arrangement of the orchestral score, in which form the work was published soon after.   Roul Pugno joined Saint-Saëns in a performance of the Scherzo for two pianofortes (Op. 87), and the concert concluded with the Septet for pianoforte, two violins, viola, violoncello, double-bass, and trumpet (Op. 65). The programme was therefore briefly representative of the art of the composer from 1875 until the date of the occasion.

In 1912 Saint-Saëns was invited by the General Association of German Musicians, which Liszt had founded fifty years earlier, to take part in the Liszt Centenary celebrations at Heidelberg.   He accepted the invitation reluctantly.   The Society admits foreigners to its membership, and years before Liszt had nominated Saint-Saëns to the membership in succession to Berlioz.   There was some disagreement between the Society and their new French member, and he only accepted their invitation to participate in the celebrations because he feared that a refusal would be attributed to entirely wrong motives. He really did not enjoy the idea of appearing, at his advanced age, beside such masters as Risler, Busoni, and Friedheim well in the zenith of their powers.

In the summer and autumn of 1913 Saint-Saëns appeared again in England. The first occasion was at Queen's Hall on June 2nd, at a Festival held in commemoration of the 75th year of his musical life, dating from the time when as a baby of two and a half years old he first experimented at the keyboard. The second appearance alluded to occurred at the Gloucester Festival, which he attended for the production of his last oratorio, " The Promised Land," written in that year.

The programme at the Festival Concert in Queen's Hall was devoted to the works of Saint-Saëns, save for a Concerto of Mozart, in which, in preference to any of his own, the master chose to appear as a soloist on the piano.

Perhaps the choice of the concerto was influenced by memories of his first concert appearance at the Sallé Pleyel. We have, on this, no definite information; but the mere fact points to a sentiment of the kind. What thoughts the event must have awakened in the mind of the aged musician!

A lifetime in the service of Art! Crowned with honour, and still juvenile and undaunted in spirit, despite the weight of years!!

The principal item from his own pen was the Symphony in C minor.

Mr. Hermann Klein presented an album, containing the signatures of prominent person-

ages in musical life in London. And the
occasion was also dignified by the reading of
an appreciative address by Sir Alexander
Mackenzie.

During the Great War the patriotism of the
master found outlet in the publication of a
small book, entitled " Germanophile " (1916),
in which he deals, from the musicians' point
of view, with German influence in France at
that time. In 1919 the " Marche Interallièe,"
Op. 155, was written; and other lesser compositions of patriotic kind, as detailed in the
Appendix.

In October of the following year he appeared
as composer and executant at a concert in the
Trocadéro, Paris, arousing his audience to a
pitch of tremendous enthusiasm. The allurement of the warmth and sunshine of Algiers,
but forty-eight hours' journey distant, made its
irresistible appeal, and he wintered there and
incidentally achieved more concert successes.

In the autumn of 1921 we again find this
marvellous old man once more in Paris, super-
intending rehearsals of a gala performance of
" Ascanio " personally. On the night of the
public performance, however, at his request,
Reynaldo Hahn wielded the bâton.

A friend who met the composer about this
time, in Paris, informs me that despite his great
age he was still practising for two hours daily
at the pianoforte.

Again he went to Algiers, and there, on December 4th, 1921, his death occurred at the age of eighty-six years and two months.

The interment took place in Paris, although there was, at first, a suggestion for a public funeral, with military honours, at Algiers.

To this great age, then, attained the baby whose chances of survival, as the offspring of a consumptive father, at the outset appeared remote, and whose energy and achievements during an unusually long and extraordinarily strenuous life would have done credit to a Hercules.

PART II

Theme I

ARTISTIC POWERS AND OUTLOOK

Commentators, from Gounod to the present day, have made a good deal of the versatility of Saint-Saëns; but why versatility should be instanced as an outstanding sign of genius is a little difficult to apprehend. Versatility is more commonly a possession of the mediocre individual.

Saint-Saëns became great because of his inherent genius, which a thoroughly sound musical education, and the well-balanced outlook upon life instilled into him by his natural guardians, enabled him to express to the full. Circumstances, including the busy, inescapable change, variety, and travel of a concert artist's life, allied to the wit and common-sense of a highly-developed intelligence, and his inherent fondness for proving things for himself, resulted in the versatility that brought such wide-spread fame during his lifetime.

His most individual works belong to the

realm of absolute music.   Of such are the
Symphony in C minor, the Trio in F, the
Sonata in C minor for violoncello and pianoforte, the Concerto in A minor for 'cello and
orchestra, and the 2nd and 4th Concertos for
pianoforte and orchestra.   They have their
root in psychological condition, and represent
his greatness as an artist.   The very much
larger output concerned with programme music
in varying phases is representative of his extraordinary abilities as a musician : and over the
works belonging to both classifications is found
his sensitive feeling for tonal colour, and his
rhythmic and melodic fertility which are as the
imprint of his genius.

It is this feeling of colour, not always
expressed by original methods, but unfailingly
correct, that drapes his lesser creations with a
shimmering garment of illusion which blinds
us, perhaps, to the commonplaceness of an
accompaniment figure; and it is the same
quality which irradiates his more erudite, and
enduring, inspirations with a light that makes
them comprehensible and appealing to the
musically untaught.   His manner is classical,
but not obtuse.

Herein lies the explanation of the wide
appeal made by his music.   It can be equally
attractive to a " Prom." audience or to that at
the Royal Philharmonic Society's concerts.
From this also is fashioned the expanse of the

target presented by the Art of Camille
Saint-Saëns to the relentless slings of the
Philistines, when they are minded to engage in
punitive attacks upon the weak points commonly existent over an extensive front.

This square-set man of middle height, self-
possessed, and confident in bearing, with a
somewhat large nose, wonderfully bright eyes,
and clear, penetrating speaking voice, was
manifestly a strong personality. Native polite-
ness and good breeding proclaimed their presence in his conduct towards others. He had
the perfect naturalness and simplicity of
manners that are usually found in the truly
great. His intellectual powers were under full
control, and his memory was perfect. Few
incidents in the course of his public life could
destroy his self-possession and determination
to carry through his engagements.

On one occasion a fall through a trap door
injured his back, but the accident did not prevent him from keeping a promise to play in an
eight-handed arrangement for piano of his
" Marche Héroïque," although the pain he
suffered prevented him from bending in
acknowledgment of the applause.

Travel and extensive reading, allied to his
active intelligence, and a sparkling, witty style
of speech, made him a brilliant and fascinating
conversationalist.

He enjoyed a discussion; and he enjoyed it

more keenly, if possible, on paper than
verbatim, although it is credible that the latter
mode of expression provided greater entertainment for his hearers, and gave less quarter to
his adversary.

Saint-Saëns' complete mastery of the
technique of his art placed the whole gamut of
emotional expression, *via* music, under his
control. Occasionally one encounters patches
of exotic colour in his scores that are blended
into the prevailing scheme with a skill that
unifies them to it, like a thicket of rhododen-
drons blooming in semi-wild luxuriance amid
sombre conifers in a Scottish Highland glen.

Early in his career he cultivated adaptability in method of expression. To quote
Gounod, " he could write at will in the style
of Rossini, Verdi, Schumann or Wagner. He
is a musician armed with every weapon; he
knows the masters by heart."

Thus, when fondness and the necessity for
travel augmented the storehouse of his imagination, and increased the supply of tints upon
his palette, he was technically able to transmute
extraneous experiences into the fabric, emotionally, of his art.

When he restricted himself to purely programme music, to music in which the emotional
appeal is secondary to the imitative suggestion
of sounds of nature, or even of machinery (see
analysis of 5th Pianoforte Concerto), or to

suggest exotic folk-song idiom, or national characteristics (see analysis of "Africa" and the Quartet for strings, Op. 112), it was his custom to work amid the surroundings, in the very locality even, that he desired to portray, musically.

When composing the majority of his works, Saint-Saëns apparently wrote ahead pretty steadily until the construction was ended. Sometimes, however, the idea and general outlines of a work were completed, mentally, before he jotted down a note of it. Other works would be constructed from a series of sketches, briefly noted in inspired moments. This latter plan is, of course, a favourite one with many composers; but evidently Saint-Saëns was less addicted to the sketch-book habit than, say, Beethoven. He seldom revised his larger works. Probably this explains the spontaneity that pervades his music, although his facility of technical resource sometimes endangers the naïveté of his melodic flow. He was no doubt wise in refraining from the meticulous polishing-up which brushes off the pristine bloom from much creative art. We may deduce the wisdom of this course from the comparative obscurity to-day of three of his operas that were re-written efforts, "Le Timbre d'Argent," "Proserpine," and "Déjanire,"— the last pieced up from the tragedy of the same name by Louis Gallet, to which he wrote the

music. In "Déjanire," by the way, he makes use of a theme, to denote the hero, Hercules, that is utilised for the same purpose in his symphonic poem, "La Jeunesse d'Hercule."

Liszt influenced the creative art of Saint-Saëns very largely. His influence spreads beyond the sphere of the symphonic poems, which are not markedly Lisztean in manner, and it began more than a dozen years before the first symphonic poem was written. There is evidence of it in the First Concerto for pianoforte and orchestra; evidence that is curiously juxtapositioned with mannerisms obviously the outcome of reading Mozart and Beethoven.

Liszt's influence is still more noticeable in the symphonic poem, "Danse Macabre," and in the last of the piano concertos, although, considered as a whole, that work is thoroughly representative of Saint-Saëns' style in programme music.

The cyclic plan of construction is another sign of Liszt's ideas that appears pretty constantly throughout the bigger works and the chamber music of Saint-Saëns. This was not, of course, a characteristic of Liszt alone. César Franck, a contemporary of both Liszt and Saint-Saëns, was greatly attracted by the plan. There is a curious affinity in emotional content, and in structural idea, although not otherwise, between the Third Symphony, in C minor, of Saint-Saëns, and that in D of

César Franck. Both are immortal works, and
both were given to the world about the same
time—1886 and 1889. The kinship of their
mood provokes thought as to what may be the
source of artistic inspiration, apart from music
that owes its being to programmatic suggestion.
It is unlikely that Franck plagiarised the idea
of Saint-Saëns' symphony when writing his
own work.

The Fifth Piano Concerto, and the Fantasia "Africa," of Saint-Saëns are conspicuous
examples of their creator's power of suggesting
his sound-picture by means of faint outlines
and sensitive colouring, rather than by the
sharp prints of direct sound photography.

He does not dispense with the latter method,
however. There are early indications of it in
"Phaéton," in the figure indicative of the
impatience of the steeds, and there is more
than a hint of it in the next symphonic poem,
"Danse Macabre," in which the craftsmanship
approaches the crude realism of Schöenberg
and Stravinsky, both outstanding figures of
to-day in the further development of this
special phase of the art of music.

Saint-Saëns was, however, happiest and
most successful when concerned with subtle
hints of "atmosphere" in his programme
music.

Consider, for example, the clever suggestion
of space, which is as invisible, and yet on occa-

sion as impressive, as music, that he manages at the outset in " Le Rouet d'Omphale." A simple device of instrumentation creates the effect. The tone of muted violins, and flutes, playing alternate bars of the figure employed, in conjunction with an abrupt change of key each time, produces the peculiar tonal colour at the beginning of the poem. Similar methods are employed in " Phaéton "; in the second part of the Third Symphony in C minor—although the application there is psychological; in the accompaniment of the song, sung by Katherine in scene 1 of the final act in " Henry VIII."; in the symphonic description of the flood in " Le Déluge "; and in the last number of " The Promised Land." Further allusion will be found in Part III. of this book to other instances of this characteristic of the composer's methods.

Undoubtedly the artistic tenets of Berlioz and Gounod became absorbed in the make-up of their young protégé, much as marked Beethoven and Mozart traits, observable in his earlier works, were submerged in his mature art.

A mannerism, partly of Liszt and partly of Chopin, sometimes obtrudes in the piano concertos. A broad melody in octaves, for right hand, may be accompanied by flowing arpeggi for left hand, with, or without, orchestral support. Typical examples of this occur in the

E

second movement of the Fifth Piano Concerto, in the first movement of the Second Piano Concerto, and in the First Sonata for violoncello and piano.

Saint-Saëns was most certainly unaware of any inheritance from Chopin—if it is an inheritance, and not merely a coincidence. Possibly a similarity in the nature of both (although there is little external indication of it) explains the unkind implications upon Chopin, as pianist and composer, which Saint-Saëns occasionally made.

In "*Au Courant de la Vie*," he tells of a dog that was fond of music, and would curl itself up, under the legs, or beside the feet, of the pianist; but that after hearing eight bars or so of any piece by Chopin the animal would get up and leave the room, with its tail between its legs!

Similarities do not invariably attract. They repel rather, when they exist between the work of two artists, especially creative artists. Saint-Saëns himself noted that circumstance in the relationship of Auber and Massenet, and it partly explained the attitude of Massenet towards Saint-Saëns.

Saint-Saëns often began his themes on the middle or last beat in the bar, and the dotted, and double-dotted, note is a characteristic of his melodic line. It appears at the beginning of his First and Second Symphonies, in the

Violin Concerto in B minor, and in the First and Second Quartets for Strings—to quote a few instances extending over the many years of his productivity. In the chamber music in particular this type of melody has often the artless lilt of a folk-song.

On the other hand, he has written a few melodies that have been inevitably harmonised *à la* chorale, as in the noble theme towards the close of Part I. of the Third Symphony. They are a complete contrast in style to his more usual manner.

When concerned with a libretto, or a definite programme, his expression has naturally been governed by extraneous suggestion, and sometimes, as in the Suite Algérienne, the extreme slightness of the thematic material does not expand beyond a melodic figure of three or four notes, often remarkably apt in suggestion.

The music of Saint-Saëns is strongly rhythmic. His independence in this characteristic has progressed consistently, until, in his middle and later periods, we find changes of time-signature, in alternate bars, or as interpolations, wherever the composer insistently felt their need.

An early indication of rhythmic freedom occurs in the Third Concerto for pianoforte and orchestra. The tendency is more strongly marked in "Henry VIII.," and in Part II. of the Third Symphony, where a really remark-

able effect is brought about as detailed in my
analysis of that work.

This intuitive anticipation of the tendency towards plastic rhythms, which is a
characteristic of the most recent music of
European nations, is an index to the genius of
Saint-Saëns.

A survey of the life-work of this remarkable
man leads to the conclusion that in colour and
rhythm his influence will be far-reaching in the
musical art of the future. In these two direc-
tions he bridges the past with the present. His
unusually long life and great productivity led
to the unusual circumstance of the development of his genius during his lifetime. He
did not belong to the pathetic band of pioneers,
in the history of the arts and sciences, whose
mortal span fell short of the length of their
spiritual missions, and whose ideas have con-
sequently had to be completed by other minds.

Saint-Saëns has not created any new form;
but under his art, symphony, symphonic poem,
concerto, opera, and oratorio progressed. The
ability to subtly mirror emotional condition
exists to an uncommon degree in his symphonic
writing, and in his chamber music, and upon
this structural foundation it is conceivable that
a new form may be built by a successor.

The master's outlook upon the progress of
musical art was somewhat bounded by the sun-
down of his own day. He expressed the view

that one might get accustomed to anything, even to bad habits, and unprepared, and unresolved, dissonances, which he likened to them.

This view was hardly charitable, and certainly lacked the breadth of outlook with which he regarded most things. In expressing himself thus, Saint-Saëns evidently overlooked the fact that his own music, to say nothing of of that of some of his precursors, would probably have sounded far from agreeable to the ears of Monteverde or Palestrina, who by their use or "invention" of the chord of the dominant seventh laid the foundations of the harmonic structure developed by their successors, including Saint-Saëns.

While holding no brief for the prophets of noise, as an art (?)—its place in science I do not question—one cannot ignore logic in considering the progress of musical art. One must listen to the results of the experiments in sound, rhythm, and polyphony, with a perfectly open mind. If the experimenters achieve their aims, they are surely worthy of commendation, whether or not their ideas call forth one's personal admiration.

Unfortunately, some ultra-modern composers appear to have no definite goal, if, indeed, they are aware of any at all. This indecision, like the frank sensationalism of others, probably caused Saint-Saëns to allude

to their efforts in the manner that he did, for
he was usually lenient, and often illuminating,
in his appreciation of the art of the contemporaries of his younger days.

His criticisms compel admiration by their
cool logic and detachment from any bias of
sentiment. His attitude, therefore, to many of
those who, as he said, were not of his day, may
be explained by the superficiality of some
modern music.

Berlioz, as we have seen, was one of the
friends of his youthful years, a friend for whom
he had a deep admiration and affection. He
was under no illusions over what he regarded
as the older master's failings as a composer.
He compares the effect of the thirty-eight
trumpets and trombones which Berlioz uses in
his " Requiem," with the manner in which
Mozart cleverly suggests, with only one trom-
bone, a similar idea; and he points out that
Berlioz, like Beethoven, had little regard for
the peculiar needs of the human voice, treat-
ing it merely as a man-made instrument. At
the same time, he directs attention to the
Olympian grandeur of conception in the
Berlioz work.

In the judgment of Saint-Saëns, Meyerbeer,
who died when the young composer was 29
years old, was a greater musician than an
artist. The famous Frenchified Berliner's
posthumous " L'Africanne " was patched to-

gether by Fétis, Perrin, and du Locle, and produced long before Saint-Saëns had made any operatic venture.

Meyerbeer's love of polish spoilt the appeal of much of his work. His fondness for creating all possible publicity in advance of the production of a new work, by announcing it long before completion, or by delaying the production on one pretext or another, certainly denoted a genius for Nineteenth Century advertising methods.

Saint-Saëns regarded Meyerbeer as an important agent in the progress of opera. He heralded the dawn of the *leit-motif* in "Robert le Diable," and at that early date (1831) also, and in "Les Huguenots," he substituted the short, distinctive prélude for the long overture.

The besetting weakness of Meyerbeer appears to have been his susceptibility to the suggestion of others, which sometimes led to the reconstruction almost of an entire opera, fashioned after the ideas of various friends.

Whether a desire for passing fame and success, or a sincere wish to perfect his work, was at the root of Meyerbeer's operatic vacillations does not concern us here. The weakness has helped to consign his work to the oblivion that is its condition to-day. Saint-Saëns expressed the charitable view of the matter.

Towards Offenbach, Saint-Saëns felt the indulgence, not unmixed with irritation, that

the master-craftsman inevitably feels for the apprentice.

Offenbach's practically inexhaustible fund of pleasing melodies, and his instinctive harmonic sense, which sometimes had surprising results—as in "Daphnïs et Chloé," where exists an early instance of the dominant eleventh—drew the commendation of Saint-Saëns. But of the amazing numerical assemblage of seventy operas left by this German Jew, who installed himself in Paris two years before the birth of Saint-Saëns, and remained there until he died in 1880, we hear nothing to-day save "Les Contés d'Hoffmann" and (lately) "The Goldsmith of Toledo"—both posthumous productions. And the former opera was finished, and corrected, by Guiraud.

The appreciation of Saint-Saëns for the genius of Liszt was whole-hearted. At a time when the art of the great pianist-composer was unpopular in Paris, he exerted himself energetically to combat the derogatory influence. He organised an orchestral concert in the Théâtre Italien, and produced the Dante Symphony, and the *Andante* from the Faust Symphony. He was greatly impressed by the beauty of the oratorio "Christus," which he heard for the first time at Heidelberg. Although he had previously gained a very high impression of the oratorio from reading the score, its many fine qualities, of conception

and technique, were revealed, when actually
heard, to an extent that far exceeded his
expectations.

The skilled use which Liszt makes in this
mighty work of the human voice in all shades
of colour, from the voices of young children to
the most sonorous *timbre* of the adult male,
excited the admiration of the French master as
much as the orchestral ensemble. He realised,
however, that occasionally Liszt appeared to
over-estimate the significance of certain quite
ordinary chordal sequences in some of his
instrumental works.

Liszt's sensitive temperamental endowment,
which gave an unapproachable distinction to
his executive art, probably led to the errors of
judgment, as a creative artist, noted by Saint-
Saëns. If Liszt had curbed his theatricality
(supposing that he could have been conscious
of it, himself), his critics of to-day would have
had greater cause for their accusations of
artificiality.

The conceptive greatness of the Sonata in
B minor, which has probably had more slight-
ing references made about it than any other
pianoforte composition of importance performed regularly in our time, was very real to
Saint-Saëns. Like a skilful physician, con-
fronted by a mysterious malady, he diagnosed
the cause, of this general lack of appreciation,
without effort. In his opinion, the technical,

or emotional, insufficiency of many of the concert pianists who essay the interpretation of the Sonata causes its subtleties to remain hidden, and brings about the misconception of the public. The combined qualities of a great artist, and of a great virtuoso, as well as an appreciation of Liszt's style, are indispensable for the presentation of the work.

Saint-Saëns admired greatly the facility of Massenet in orchestrating his works, for Massenet was able to turn out page after page of orchestration with little apparent effort; and the gracefulness, and prevalent gaiety of it, also attracted him.

He envied the success that followed Massenet's nice judgment of the taste and sympathies of his operatic public. This power amounted to an extra sense in Jules Massenet. He possessed it in greater degree than Saint-Saëns, who was the greater artist of the two.

One of the penalties imposed upon those born during the present phase of civilisation is the constant misunderstanding of the purest motives, to which the prevalence of sophistry, and the religion of self-seeking, leads.

At heart Massenet apparently regarded Saint-Saëns' friendly advances with suspicion, and in a spirit of professional rivalry. Each publicly acclaimed his admiration for the other, but fear of a private friendship being turned to professional uses, hindered any real inti-

macy. Their relationship was thus interesting,
but pathetic.

In contrast to this sad picture of the devastating results which the conventional outlook may
breed, we have one of the very charming, and
trustful, friendship that existed between Saint-
Saëns and Bizet.

They were fellow-students, striving together
to gain the public ear in the same profession;
fellow-confidants of each other's hopes, joys,
and sorrows; and mutual judges, and encour-
agers, of each other's art. The picture, limited
in scope by the tragically early death of
Bizet, became as an exquisite memory to
Saint-Saëns.

Happy also was the relationship of Saint-
Saëns with Delibés, who was a year his junior,
and who eventually became a director of the
Opéra, and a professor at the Conservatoire—
Delibés, who longed to write grand opera, and
who had to content himself with writing ballets.
Saint-Saëns regarded his "Coppélia" as a
marvellous work.

Ernest Guiraud, another member of this early
quartet of student friends, also developed as
a composer of opera, and taught composition
at the Conservatoire. Saint-Saëns held him in
much esteem, and affection, and he was responsible for the piano scores of several of Saint-
Saëns' operas. As related elsewhere, the
master undertook the onerous duty of com-

pleting Guiraud's opera "Frédégonde," in 1895, in an attempt to add posthumous fame to his name three years after his death.

Saint-Saëns' admiration for Wagner was tempered with a feeling that sometimes the older master tended towards harmonic excesses; but in the main his praise was unstinted. "Die Meistersinger" and "Die Walküre" called forth his highest eulogiums. Wagner, as recorded in Part I., openly expressed his admiration of Saint-Saëns' superb musicianship, and of his powers as a composer.

Auber and Saint-Saëns were intimately acquainted. The elderly composer (he was fifty-three years the senior of Saint-Saëns) interested himself in his promising young countryman, of whom he was fond. He had considerable influence in Paris and was instrumental in starting Saint-Saëns upon his operatic career. But it is rather odd that Auber did not procure for his young friend a libretto from Scribe, who was the most popular librettist of the day, and the man whose collaboration helped so greatly in the success of Auber's own operas (he wrote over forty), and who also gained distinction with Meyerbeer.

Saint-Saëns had little regard for the music of Brahms, who was two years his senior. He considered that many people mistook the heaviness of Brahms' music for depth; but it is a little surprising that the Hambourger's

chamber works did not appeal to Saint-Saëns'
love of academic style in that form of music.

His friendship with Rubinstein, and his
meeting with Tschaikowsky (whose music was
naturally sympathetic to him) have already been
alluded to, like his friendship with Rossini.

It was at the *salon* of Rossini, in the Chausée
d'Antin that Adelina Patti, then lacking in her
artistic sense and judgment of later years, in-
curred the displeasure of the great Italian by
taking unwarrantable liberties with the aria from
" Le Barbier." She altered it so much in performance, that after complimenting her upon
her beautiful voice, Rossini asked her the name
of the composer of the aria !

In the opinion of Saint-Saëns, Rossini wrote
nothing of value after " Guillaume Tell."

The hostility which forced him to seek the
semi-privacy of the life in the *appartement* in
the Chausée d'Antin stopped the flow of adula-
tion, which was so necessary to make the foun-
tain of his inspiration shoot forth its brilliant jets.

Richard Strauss was forty-eight when Saint-
Saëns saw him at Heidelberg, in 1912, at the
Liszt Centenary Celebrations. He formed a
high opinion of Strauss' powers as a conductor,
and of his possibilities as a force in the evolution of musical art. The most recent examples
of Strauss' creative art do not support this
prognostication, and his powers as a conductor,
to-day, are more adequate than inspired.

Among the pupils of Saint-Saëns attention may be directed to the names of Gabriel Fauré, André Messager, and Arthur de Greef.

To appreciate clearly the part played by Saint-Saëns in the development of musical art, and establish a sense of perspective, it is necessary to recollect that at the time he began his career as a composer, with the symphony dedicated to Seghers, *i.e.*, when he was seventeen years of age, the later string quartets of Beethoven were regarded as revolutionary and more or less unplayable, by Parisian musicians.

PART II

Theme II

SOCIAL LIFE AND OPINIONS

In his own individual manner, and especially in connection with his art, Saint-Saëns found much interest in social life. He had a child-like ability for finding joy and pleasure in simple things that must surely have contributed largely to the preservation of the clarity of intellectual powers, and freshness, which are found even in his latest creative work.

The ability is one that is often present in the personality of genius, and doubtless has its function as a compensating action for the otherwise severe strain to which the nervous system of a highly-specialised human organisation is subjected. When it does not exist, the genius, that is proverbially akin to madness, crosses the border-line. As an example of that kind of catastrophe one recollects the end of Schumann's life, Victor Hugo's decline, and the weakness that is said to have threatened Liszt during the illness which preceded the attack of

pneumonia that swiftly gathered him to the sickle of the grim Reaper.

I am indebted to a friend, Mme. Amina Goodwin, the distinguished pianist, for the following incidents which serve to illustrate this youthful trait in the personality of Saint-Saëns. Mme. Amina Goodwin knew the master intimately, and it was through him (as the third incident, published in the " Morning Post " of 27.12.21, shows), that she came to know Liszt. *En passant,* it is of interest to record that this fine artist also began her professional career when she was a mere child, and that it brought her into association with Brahms, Pugno, and other notabilities in the musical world.

I quote the incidents just as related by my informant :

" M. Léon Glaize, a well-known portrait painter of Lille, was a great friend of Saint-Saëns, from the time when they were both very young. They used to have weekly ' Musical Evenings ' with Pugno (the great pianist), in Glaize's painting studio. These were very merry evenings for all concerned.

" Saint-Saëns improvised the music of a comedy, called ' La Blouse et l'Habit,' or, ' Le fils de la Revolution.' There was a flood, and a fire, in this play, and the music was most descriptive of these exciting disasters. The words were written by Paul Ferrier, in conjunction with Paul Devoulède.

"Mme. Glaize, the mother of the painter, was also a friend of Saint-Saëns' dear old mother. Glaize painted the portrait of Saint-Saëns, life size, and it was greatly admired in the *Salon* of Paris, 1899. This portrait now hangs in the Maison Erard, in Paris.

"At a great festival, in the North of France, given in honour of Camille Saint-Saëns, the President naturally begged the composer to be present at the big dinner given on the occasion. Saint-Saëns replied that to his great regret he could not possibly dine out, having to follow a very strict diet. The President assured him that he could be served with whatever dish he wanted. The composer then explained that the doctor had ordered him to eat the glutinous, and nutritious, part of pigs' feet. 'All right!' replied the President, 'You shall have pigs' feet!'

"The day of the banquet, which was a very sumptuous affair, arrived, and Saint-Saëns was served with the much-discussed dish of pigs' feet. As the composer was a bit of a *gourmét*, and always enjoyed a good dinner, he was sorely tempted by all the delicious courses handed round, but did not dare touch any rich food. At last he could stand it no longer, and there was a marked *crescendo* in his temper as he battled with the dish of pigs' feet. Having finished it, he suddenly rose from the table, flushed with anger, and in spite of the protesta-

F

tions, and prayers, of the President and the other guests, insisted upon leaving the banquet, notwithstanding the fact that the whole affair had been given in the composer's honour." (This incident is very typical of Saint-Saëns' impulsive, and child-like nature.)

From " The Morning Post," 27.12.21 :—

" Miss Amina Goodwin, the well-known founder of the London Trio, writes concerning her memory of Camille Saint-Saëns in the following terms :—

" ' Although a considerable amount of musical matter and appreciation has been written the last few days about the late eminent composer, Saint-Saëns, a few lines of personal remembrance of the man may not be without interest. The first thing that struck me was his devotion to his mother, which was very beautiful.

" ' When I went to his house in Paris, as a child (having won a scholarship at the Paris Conservatoire), he would not let me leave, after playing to him one of his piano works, until he had taken me into another room to see his dear mother, to whom he told all the details of my visit.

" ' Saint-Saëns was ever ready to give a helping hand to his colleagues, and was deeply appreciative to artists who interpreted his music to his satisfaction. When I expressed a timid wish for a few lines to his friend Liszt, before going to Weimar, the kindest letter was at once forthcoming.

"'After Liszt had read it he came forward, exclaiming, "Ah! Mon cher Saint-Saëns," and greeted me with the same warmth and affection as his thoughts for his great friend and admirer evoked.

"'On one occasion, after a slight misunderstanding, his impatience caused me to dissolve into tears. He at once patted my head and apologised for his hastiness. His disposition was impulsive to a degree, but he had a great sense of humour and wit.

"'He was highly amused one day at Broadwood's (then in Great Pulteney Street), where he came to hear me rehearse his well-known "Variations for two pianos" on a theme of Beethoven, which I was going to play, with Max Pauer, at a recital for two pianos. When he saw the enormous height of Max Pauer standing next to "little me," his amusement was intense. Saint-Saëns exclaimed "That will not do," and lifted me on to a chair, which, as I stood on it, brought my head to the same level as that of Max. "Voila, c'est mieux, now you are as tall as your colleague."

"'Truly, Saint-Saëns had a charming and child-like nature, allied to deep sincerity and depth of character.'"

The charm of manner which attracted the friendship of so many famous artists to Saint-Saëns made him a favourite with the many Royal personages with whom he came into

touch. To mention the Royalties of the 'eighties and 'nineties whom Saint-Saëns did *not* meet would be simpler than to relate anecdotes, and refer to all those whom he knew. In his " École Buissonière " he relates his experiences in the inimitable fashion that is distinctively his. The following anecdotes are abridgements therefrom :

He was received in audience twice by Queen Victoria at Windsor Castle. On the first of these occasions he was presented by a friend, the Baroness de Caters, who was, at that time, giving lessons in singing to the Princess Beatrice, then a bashful young girl.

The audience was an informal one, and when Her late Majesty entered the room she came forward with both hands extended in cordial welcome. Saint-Saëns afterwards played to her upon the organ (in the chapel at Windsor) and upon the piano. Finally, he accompanied the Princess as she sang the aria from " Étienne Marcel."

Queen Victoria was so delighted that some days after, without the composer being told of it, she summoned to Windsor Madame Gye (*i.e.*, Madame Albani-Gye), wife of the manager of Covent Garden, to ask to have " Étienne Marcel " staged at her own theatre. The Queen's wish, for a reason which Saint-Saëns does not state, was not granted.

The second audience was accorded to the

composer seventeen years later. The Queen
was then unable to walk alone, and Saint-Saëns
expresses himself as having felt heart-broken at
the change in her appearance. However, once
seated at a small table she seemed much as
before, excepting for her white hair.

She asked the composer about " Henry
VIII.," which was being given for the second
time at Covent Garden, and he told her about
his manuscript find in the library at Buckingham Palace, and of the use which he had made
of the Sixteenth Century air in the opera.
Queen Victoria was much interested, and
His Highness the Duke of Connaught wrote
Saint-Saëns that she spoke of it several times.

Altogether charming is the account given by
Saint-Saëns of the audience granted him by Her
Majesty Queen Alexandra. She received him
along with Joseph Hollman, the violoncellist.

On this occasion Queen Alexandra was in
deep mourning for the successive deaths of her
parents, the King and Queen of Denmark. She
spoke to Saint-Saëns about her mother, whom
he had met at Copenhagen with her sisters, the
Dowager Empress of Russia, and the Princess
of Hanover, and was cordial in her manner.
After he had played a duet with Hollman,
Queen Alexandra expressed a desire to hear
him play alone. As he attempted to lift the lid
of the instrument, the Queen stepped forward
to help him to raise it before her maids of

honour (Lady Gray and the Hereditary Princess of Greece) could intervene. Queen Alexandra afterwards presented to each of the artists, in the name of herself and of His late Majesty King Edward VII., who was absent, a gold medal commemorative of artistic merit, and she offered them a cup of tea which she had herself poured out. The composer's account of the reception gives a delightful picture of the gracious lady who is so dear to the hearts of the British people to-day.

Queen Christine of Spain, who had heard Saint-Saëns play the piano, expressed a desire to hear him play the organ. Arrangements were therefore made for him to play to her in a church, upon a certain day. Some great ladies of the period lectured the indiscreet Queen for daring to resort to a church for any purpose other than that of taking part in Divine Service.

In response, Queen Christine, instead of going privately to the church to hear the master play, attended in great state, with King Alphonso (who was then very young), with the Ministers and the Court, while horsemen, stationed at intervals along the Royal route, blew trumpets!

Saint-Saëns had written a religious march specially for the occasion, and the Queen graciously accepted the dedication. Then she asked him to play " Mon cœur s'ouvre à ta voix," from " Samson et Dalila." While, con-

siderably flustered at the request in such a place, he hurriedly improvised an organ arrangement of the aria, and the Queen listened, with an expression of rapt attention, her elbow on the keyboard and her chin resting on one hand. One can only express the utmost admiration for the independent conduct of the Royal lady.

Queen Amelie of Portugal once honoured the composer by according to him a quite informal reception. She dispensed with all her ladies-in-waiting, for the occasion, which enabled her to have her guest sit in a chair near to her and enjoy a chat upon various topics.

In his account of his friendship with Their Majesties the King and Queen of the Belgians, whom he first knew when they were heirs-apparent, there is a delightful little incident relating to Queen Elizabeth. One day, in addressing her in conversation, the aged composer forgot, for the moment, her accession in rank, and spoke to her as " Highness "; then, remembering, apologised for his mistake. The Queen replied, with a smile, " Don't apologise," said she, " that recalls good times."

The life of Saint-Saëns is one of unusual interest even for the individual not deeply interested in the art of music, for he met so many interesting people, distinguished in literature, science, and pictorial art during the course of his long life.

The fact that his mother was an amateur painter (apparently she painted chiefly portraits) served to bring him into close contact with many of the leading artists of his day. Some of his mother's pictures are exhibited in the Musée de Saint-Saëns at Dieppe.

Ingres, who is known to the public of this decade by reproductions of his picture, "La Source," was credited with skill as a violinist by popular report; but Saint-Saëns, who knew him intimately from childhood, contradicted any such idea. In reply to a direct enquiry, Ingres informed his young friend, in a vague manner, that he had once played second violin in a string quartet. His opinions on musical art of the period were echoes of the views of Delsarte, and of Henri Reber, and his knowledge of music was not gained, apparently, from practical experience, although his love for the art was unquestionable. According to the composer, Ingres was a rather serious old man, inclined to profundity, and (one suspects) something of a poseur in matters of taste. But he apparently exerted a strong influence, in firing the ambitions of the small boy, at an early age.

Saint-Saëns met Gustave Doré at the *salon* of Rossini, where he was a frequent visitor, and belonged to the *dilletanti* who championed the cause of melody and opposed "learned scientific music." The two became friends, visited

each other frequently, and discussed questions
of the day as well as their own private affairs.
Doré finally made the composer the confidant
of his innermost thoughts. Apparently jovial
and boyish, he was in reality melancholy, and
sensitive, lacking in commonsense application
of his artistic powers (that could hardly have
been otherwise, considering his imaginative
qualities) and inclined to attribute the failure
of his paintings to prejudice and spite rather
than to the fulsome appreciation of the press
for his art as a designer. He had a most wonderful memory for visualising detail, and he
preferred to rely upon it and disdained the use
of models, which was a disastrous plan in the
painting of large pictures. Saint-Saëns records
having seen Doré engaged upon work on thirty
canvasses at a time in his studio.

Doré could play the violin with a certain
amount of technical proficiency, and had he
worked at acquiring a technique would probably
have been a successful artist in that direction
also, for he had undoubted temperament, and
good taste, and an unusual natural aptitude.
But if he could not master a piece immediately
he at once gave up trying to play it. The loss
of his mother, from whom he had never been
separated, aggravated a heart affection and
brought about his own death.

The friendship which existed between Saint-
Saëns and Henri Regnault has already been

described in Part I. of this book. Saint-Saëns never ceased to regret the suppression of certain portions of some letters to the painter when they were published after his death, and which related to Regnault's high opinion of his friend's music. Professional rivalry was at the root of these editorial excisions; but as the master very sensibly pointed out, the opinions could have harmed the artistic prestige of nobody, coming from an artist in another profession, and biased, as they obviously were, by the mutual love of the friends. And so Saint-Saëns, himself, created a monument to that friendship—his " Marche Héroïque," which, in its original orchestral garb, and in the form of transcriptions, he frequently had performed during his lifetime. Regnault had an exquisite tenor voice, and was, moreover, a cultured musician.

After the performance of the " Hymne à Victor Hugo," which renewed the friendship between Saint-Saëns and Hugo, and which was given at the grand reception at the Trocadéro planned to honour the great man, Saint-Saëns was invited to dine with him, and thereafter was a frequent guest at the house.

In his " École Buissonière " Saint-Saëns describes, at length, his relationship with Victor Hugo. I quote below from the English translation of part of that book (" Musical Memories," John Murray), as the phraseology

of the intimate picture of Hugo's family life,
given by the composer, is so good :—
" I often dined with him informally, with M. and Mme.
Lockroy, Meurice, Vacquerie, and other close friends.
The fare was delightful and unpretentious, and the conversation was the same. The master sat at the head of
the table, with his grandson and grand-daughter at either
side, saying little, but always something *à propos*. Thanks
to his vigour, his strong, sonorous voice, and his quiet
good humour, he did not seem like an old man, but rather
like an ageless and immortal human being, whom Time
would never touch. His presence was just Jove-like
enough to inspire respect, without chilling his followers."

In the opinion of Saint-Saëns the artist is
entitled to explore all avenues of emotional
and psychological experience in pursuit of his
art, and to work towards his chosen goal in the
manner that seems, to him, best. But this line
of conduct should not be regarded as in any
sense a duty. It is a privilege, to be made use
of when need demands. One might find an
analogy between the social position of the music
student (or student of any art for that matter)
towards humanity in general, and that of the
medical student (or other science student). The
work and research of both is for the ultimate
good, and happiness, of humanity.

Without hard work, and constant application,
he did not think that any artist, however boun-
teous his natural endowments might be, could
ever become really great : could ever advance
his art (and, incidentally, civilisation) a single
step in the evolutionary process. For that, and

not the plaudits of the multitude, is the mission, and the acid test, of great achievement, whether applied to art, science, religion, or even politics.

The artist who can cover the entire field of his own particular art has not yet been born. That is an opinion that was held by the subject of this volume, and constitutes, I consider, the best refutation that can be made of the irritating and entirely untrue custom, due to slovenly thought, which certain writers on the art of Saint-Saëns have formed, of stating that his great claim to consideration lies in his all-round excellence.

The art of Saint-Saëns reveals notable failures, as well as splendid triumphs. A reference to Part III. will, I think, demonstrate this, and the fact of their existence is a sign of his genius. Genius oft-times rushes in where ordinary mortals fear to tread. Sometimes, like a skilfully-managed aeroplane, it soars into the empyrean blue; and sometimes, like the man-made instrument of flight, it gets out of control, dashes earthwards, and meets disaster. But it never plays for safety. It is manipulated by invisible levers.

Saint-Saëns considered that there was room for artists of all kinds, owing to the vastness of the domain of music. For, indeed, music is bound up with most conditions of life, and musicians of varying abilities may find each his special *metier*.

There is the music of simple kind, the function of which is an amusement; the music connected with ceremonies, with birth, marriage, and death; that which is associated with the message of religion, or intensifies the appeal of the art of the dramatist, and the poet; there is the music of Nature, and the worker; and that which exercises the highest office of all, by stirring the quiescent divinity in humanity.

The master expressed the view that the cinema, like the concert, should be used as a factor in education. That by means of the moving picture science, and art, might be shown to the public in their true relationship to everyday life, and as the foundational principles to which it is beholden for the amenities of civilised life which it enjoys, and accepts, as a matter of course. By this dictum he did not, I think, pretend to originality—for he was thoroughly conversant with current schools of thought—but merely desired to emphasise a truth.

He voices this opinion regarding music for the masses ("Musical Memories"):—

"Music holds so high a place in the modern world that we ought to begin with that. There is plenty of gay music, easy to understand, which is in harmony with the laws of art, and the people ought to hear it instead of the horrors which they cram into our ears under the pretence of satisfying our tastes.

"What pleases people most is sentimental music, but it need not be a silly sentimentality. Instead, they ought

to give the people the charming airs which grow as naturally as daisies on a lawn in the vast field of opéra-comique.

" That is not high art, it is true, but it is pretty music, and it is high art compared with what is heard too often in the cafés. I am not ignorant of the fact that such establishments employ talented people. But along with the good, what frightful things one hears ! And no one would listen to their instrumental repertoire anywhere else !

" . . . . very often, even at the theatres, the managers satisfy their own tastes under the pretence of satisfying that of the public. That is, of course, intensely human. We judge others by ourselves."

This is a good, and eminently practical, doctrine for spreading the appreciation, and knowledge, of the best music. Just as the child must learn to walk, before he can run, so must the musically untaught individual be gradually accustomed to an appreciation of the structural beauties, and intellectual value, of music on its highest plane. Its emotional service will then be enduring, instead of the transitory—if pleasurable—"exhalation of art," to which Victor Hugo likened it.

PART III

THE CONCERTOS

The writing of works for a solo instrument and orchestra was a form of musical composition much favoured by Saint-Saëns. If we regard the list of works belonging to this class enumerated in the Appendix, we find that there are twenty to which, in this broad sense, the name "Concerto" might be applied. Some of them represent the work of the composer in its most inspired and characteristic vein, and display his constructive ability at its best.

Following, I shall discuss the compositions that adhere in general detail to the accepted ideas of a concerto, *i.e.*, briefly, symphonic works of three or four movements which have an important part assigned to a solo instrument.

Remembering the master's earliest associations with music, and his favourite rôle as an executant, it is quite in the natural sequence of development that his five concertos for pianoforte and orchestra should occupy an important place in his creative output.

Concerto No. 1, *Op.* 17, *in D* (1858-9, *published* 1875), *for pianoforte and orchestra. Dedicated to Mme. Alfred Jaël.*

This early concerto shows clearly the influence of Mozart (first movement) and Beethoven (second movement); but it is also individual to the extent of the very copious passage work, in scales and arpeggi, for the solo instrument, which is characteristic of its successors. The influence of earlier masters even is discernible in the melodic outline and accompaniment figures.

The *Andante* commences with a subdued hunting-call theme, on the brass, that might have been lifted from a Mozart sonata. But even then, the Saint-Saëns of the future peeps forth in several bars of cadenza of a strongly individual kind.

The second movement, *Andante sostenuto quasi adagio* (the composer of twenty-four was apparently particular about gradations of emotional condition !), contains a very beautiful theme that is dealt with, variazioni, and with interjections of cadenza to the extent of cheapness of effect. The orchestra has little to say, and the movement is in the nature of an intermezzo.

The third movement, *Allegro con fuoco*, is, as pointed out, Beethovenish. There is an exquisitely pleading, secondary theme that finally gains the ascendancy and triumphs over

the trumpery first subject. During the transition it acquires ethereal beauty, as announced on the wood-wind over a ceaseless, running commentary of arpeggi, upon the piano. Here, indeed, is a suggestion of Liszt, whose constructive methods began to insinuate themselves upon the young composer's artistic vista some six years previously.

Concerto No. 2, Op. 22, in G minor, for pianoforte and orchestra (1868). *Dedicated to Mme. A. de Villers, née de Haber.*

The first movement, *Andante sostenuto*, has a long cadenza for the solo instrument with arpeggi over a tonic pedal 8va G, over the whole expanse of the keyboard, from bottom to top, then descends, and ascends, in a bravura scale passage (G minor) in fifths, succeeded by three declamatory chords of the seventh. To this succeeds more arpeggi, followed by chordal passages over an octave pedal. After two bars of prelude, by pianoforte, the orchestra enters on a sustained tonic chord, for brass and wood-wind. The first theme :—

of heroic, and elevated, mood, is then stated

G

by the piano, first as a melody over a flowing accompaniment for the left hand.

This theme undergoes considerable amplification, growing in intensity and passion, and there are conversational passages between the solo instrument and the strings, and showy scale passages in octaves, for solo, before a plaintive theme

Pfe. Con. Nº 2. Op. 22. in G minor

of syncopated rhythm is announced on the pianoforte.

Afterwards comes the brilliant working out, supported chiefly by sustained chords for the strings, parts of the opening theme being heard in various sections of the orchestra. The theme is again heard in octaves (*p.*) for the right hand of the soloist, with arpeggi for the left hand.

Arpeggi sweep up and down the keyboard, and through this wealth of colour, in rising crescendo, is heard an impression of the theme, high in the wood-wind, before a cadenza for piano, and a recapitulation, which includes the pedal and arpeggi preludial matter, brings the movement to a triumphant conclusion, *tutti*.

The second movement, *Allegro scherzando*, is airily graceful in character, and one of the

most charming ever written. It is in six-eight time throughout, and the colour impression of ethereal elusiveness is created at the outset by the scoring for the strings, *pizzicato*, while tympani denote the rhythm. At bar 5 the pianoforte enters with a theme

of an elfin capriciousness, a veritable Danse de Puck. This is gaily bandied about between the solo instrument and the various sections of the orchestra, modulation assisting in the variety of colour obtained.

A bridge scale passage brings the piano to an accompaniment figure of rocking rhythm, reminiscent of the twanging of a seranading guitar. The melody of this is given out by the bassoon, supported by the lower strings. Soon the entire orchestra is permeated by the infectious gaiety. The other instruments subside, save for a rhythmic *pizzicato* on the lower strings, and the piano gives its version of the serenade.

The rhythm of this theme is so compelling that I have heard audiences, even of the best-regulated brands, tapping their feet *pp.* in sympathy with the musicians!

The music at this part is not very far removed
from the border line that separates good,
healthy music from the blatantly vulgar. From
such a fate it is saved by the abrupt and very
effective modulation of the complementary
phrase.   One need not say much more about
this movement.   These two themes, under
various guises, represent the substance of it.

The third movement, *Presto*, opens with a
brisk rhythm of quaver triplets in common time.
The thematic material is slight. The principal
theme is a lively tarantella, with a subsidiary
theme, generally heard in unisons, that provides
an effective contrast.   The chief interest lies
with the solo instrument, the orchestral writing
being often merely a filling-in.   But the pace is
maintained and the work comes to a rousing
conclusion.

Concerto No. 3, Op. 29, *in E flat* (1869,
published 1875), *for pianoforte and orchestra.*
Dedicated to M. E. M. Delaborde.

This concerto is seldom, if ever, played now.
The mood is often inchaotic, but not morose,
and when the exceedingly vigorous third
movement is reached (*Allegro non troppo*), a
condition of almost blatant optimism becomes
supreme.

The Third Pianoforte Concerto opens,
Moderato assai, with a rippling figure, in
arpeggio demi-semiquavers, for the pianoforte,

pp. After a few bars a suave melody rises above this, on the brass and wood-wind, being allotted to the various instruments according to pitch. In due course the strings re-inforce the wind, and the soloist is ceaselessly busied with arpeggi and scale passages which culminate in a richly-coloured *molto crescendo* in passages of chromatic chords which lead to a flamboyant *Allegro maestoso*. A curious theme, *Moderato assai* (*molto tranquillo quasi ritenuto a piacere*), is ushered in in unisons, by the piano. The rhythm is unusual. In a bar of four-four one finds

alternating with normal bars in groups of four semiquavers. A brilliant development ensues, and a recapitulation, on classical lines, is rounded off by a coda and cadenzas.

The second movement, *Andante*, is neither long nor particularly arresting, and serves as an intermezzo between the chaotic and striving mood of the first movement, and the brisk, dance rhythm of the last.

The third movement, *'Allegro non troppo*, is an energetic march in two-four which is treated *con variazioni*, and contributes greatly to the verve and effective ending of the concerto.

Altogether, the general character of this work is superficial, but there are many shallower compositions, such as the Weber "Concertstücke," whose *raison d'être* in concert repertoires is the opportunity which they offer for technical displays of apparent difficulty.

Concerto No. 4, Op. 44, in C minor (1875, published 1877), for pianoforte and orchestra. Dedicated to M. Antoine Door, Professor of Pianoforte at the Vienna Conservatoire.

Deeper emotions than one commonly finds in the pianoforte works of the master pervade this concerto. The mood is predominantly tragic; first in the dumb, helpless manner that arises from an unexpected, and poignantly hopeless, sorrow, and then with the succeeding transitory stages of passionate revulsion, dull resignation, a gleam of spiritual hope, and attempts to forget, leading to the creation of a more heroic, a calmer, and a loftier state.

Under the stress of his emotion, the composer forgets to scintillate in his customary manner, via a plentiful assortment of devices for technical display on the pianoforte. Instead, one finds that the embroidery used is a natural outcome of the prevailing mood of stress and inward questioning.

The method of construction (cyclic) shows a continuity of emotional conception throughout the entire work.

The sorrowful questioning theme

with which the *Allegro moderato* opens on the violins, accompanied *pizzicato* by the lower strings, and soon amplified to a passionate climax on the pianoforte, is frequently heard during about two-thirds of the concerto, which is divided into two parts.

There is also in Part 1 another binding figure—

with which the *Allegro moderato* opens on the

a short, chromatic theme of two phrases, which is used at the opening of the *Allegro vivace* of Part 2. Homogeneity is further aided by the

use, throughout, of an exquisite chorale-like subject,

which, speaking first of resignation, in a steady rhythm, undergoes metamorphosis, and towards the end of the final *Allegro* is heard as an expression of heroic triumph, played first in single notes in three-four time (unlike the four-four of the original entry) by the pianist's right hand.

Part 1 consists of the *Allegro moderato* and an *Andante;* Part 2 of an *Allegro vivace* and *Andante,* and the final *Allegro,* the movements being continuous excepting for the break between the two parts.

This beautiful concerto is clearly absolute music.   It is of Saint-Saëns' best, and that says much.

Concerto No. 5, Op. 103, *in F, for pianoforte and orchestra* (1896). *Dedicated to M. Louis Diémer.*

The last of the pianoforte concertos begins quietly with a sustained chord of the tonic, for

the wood-wind, against an ascending passage, *pizzicato*, for strings. The solo instrument enters with a statement of the principal theme, calm, reflective, and chorale-like in mood. This is repeated in the upper section of the orchestra by the strings and wood-wind, while the solo instrument is busied with decorative arpeggios. An ascending scale passage in sixths leads to a figure that is much used throughout the movement.

Pfte Con. Nº 5. Part I. Op. 103. in F

There is a second theme, *Dolce un poco rubato*, graceful and languorous at first, and then growing in animation until a *cadenza* of broken chords leads to an emphatic declamatory figure and a resumption, *a tempo*, of the brilliant passage work in sixths, and characteristic figure, for solo, already alluded to.

Thus, in the principal subject-matter of this somewhat long movement the music alternates in mood between the calmly reflective and the amorously agitated, and the tonal colour is rich, varied, and free from turgidity.

The second movement, *Andante* (three-four),

is strongly charged with impressions of the environment of the Nile.

An irregular rhythmic figure appears to set the pace of bustle and movement on a steamboat; above the din one hears a strident melody

shrilly sung by some Arab carriers. The boat glides out upon the calm waterway. From a distance is wafted a fragment of a plaintive little air—

The mood becomes serious. There are passages of a recitative character, and gorgeous rich chords, strongly reminiscent of a rhapsody of Liszt. Then the boatmen sing a barcarolle, a flowing cantabile melody in two-four over an accompaniment in arpeggi. This continues for some time, both in the writing for solo instru-

ment and in various sections of the orchestra, and then there is an amusing sound picture of the movement of the propeller, and a piquant little strophe, a little impertinent, is heard for a brief spell. A long passage, *à la cadenza*, for pianoforte, presages a resumption of the opening rhythm, and the movement, after transitions of *tempo* and mood, almost as varied as those of the first movement, ends *pianissimo*.

In the third movement, *Molto allegro* (two-four), save for a roll on the tympani, the pianoforte enters alone with a vigorous and barbaric theme of rhythmic insistence.

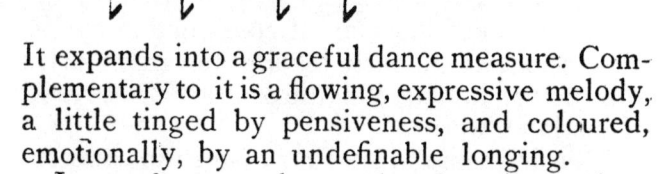

It expands into a graceful dance measure. Complementary to it is a flowing, expressive melody, a little tinged by pensiveness, and coloured, emotionally, by an undefinable longing.

In one form or other, and undergoing various modulations, these themes pervade the movement. The vigorous mood triumphs, and the concerto concludes with an orchestral *tutti* that is a blaze of colour.

This is a gracious and delightful work, at the

popularity of which, both with the public and with *virtuosi*, one cannot marvel. The last movement in particular abounds in opportunities for technical triumphs, both digitally and tonally for the pianist, and the concerto, in this respect,could hardly have been conceived by a composer who was not himself a great pianist.

Saint-Saëns has left, to the world, three concertos for violin and orchestra. The third, in B minor, is the only one that is much played to-day. It rivals the Second Piano Concerto in popularity.

Concerto No. 1, *Op.* 20 (1859, *published* 1868, *in A, for violin and orchestra. Dedicated to M. Sarasate.*

This early concerto is a comparatively brief work consisting of an *Allegro*, an *Andante espressivo*, and an *Allegro* the material of which bears considerable relationship to that in the first and makes the plan of construction cyclic. Thus is shown an early leaning towards a style of structure favoured by the composer in several of his later works.

A virile theme in six-four opens the concerto on the solo volin, after a chord, *tutti*. There is a subsidiary theme, a trifle Espagñole, melodically, and these, embellished in various ways, comprise the substance of the movement. There is much double stopping and *cadenza* passages before a prolonged trill leads into the *Andante*

espressivo, all too brief, perhaps, in its simple beauty.

The orchestration is straightforward to the point of barrenness, and there is little trace of chromaticism throughout this elegant composition.

Concerto No. 3, Op. 61, in B minor (1880, *published* 1881), *for violin and orchestra. Dedicated to Mons. P. Sarasate.*

The Third Concerto for violin and orchestra enjoys a popularity with solo violinists and the public that is not exceeded by the violin concertos of any other composers.

There is, indeed, nothing to wonder at in this. To explain the attraction, tersely, one need only regard the wealth of melody presented by its thematic material; its perpetual "aliveness," and the opportunities for virtuosic display which abound in it.

The first movement is headed *Allegro non troppo*, and a few introductory bars, *pp.*, precede the statement of the principal theme, *forte* and *appassionato*, by the solo violin. This theme is so familiar that it need be no more than indicated by excerpt here.

This passionate challenge is thrown out against an orchestral background, lightly sketched in, and at its conclusion there is some brilliant double-stopping for the soloist. There is a contrasting theme of tranquil mood that serves to enhance the glowing colour of the first subject ere it re-appears, brightly decorated with arpeggi, double-stopping, and trills, ere the movement comes to an end.

The slow movement, *Andantino quasi allegretto*, is certainly one of the most ethereally beautiful ever penned by the master. It is like the echo of a song, wafted across the expanse of a peaceful lake, from a little boat drifting idly, with its freight of youth, towards the setting sun. It is a care-free barcarolle, languorous in its happiness,

Vln. Con. Nº 3. Op. 61, in B minor

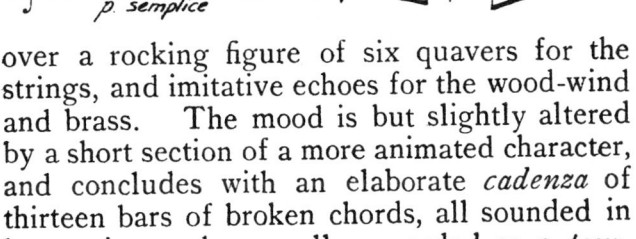

over a rocking figure of six quavers for the strings, and imitative echoes for the wood-wind and brass. The mood is but slightly altered by a short section of a more animated character, and concludes with an elaborate *cadenza* of thirteen bars of broken chords, all sounded in harmonics, and generally regarded as a *tour-de-force* technically. Poetically, the effect is

of a most gradual evaporation of sound as the little boat drifts out of sight.

The third movement, *Molto moderato e maestoso*, is full of life and virile force, and the warmth of Southern skies. The solo instrument enters with a passionate throb that is like a smouldering fire, ready to burst into a fierce flame at the slightest encouragement—

Soon we have a motive that will not be denied the happiness of life, and is alternately assertive and cajoling—

Then victory—

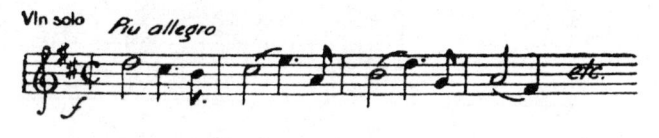

victory that is intoxicated with the ecstasy of reciprocated passion; victory that sweeps onwards in arrogant indifference, to whatever life may still hold, because it believes it has found love.

There are two concertos for violoncello and orchestra. The first is an early work, and was dedicated by the young composer to a friend, a 'cellist, much his senior, whom he held in great esteem.

Concerto No. 1, Op. 33, for violoncello and orchestra, in A minor (1872, *published* 1873). *Dedicated to M. Auguste Tolbecque.*

There is a fresh spontaneity about this concerto, and a sureness of touch, that probably explains the popularity which it enjoys. It may be of interest to mention that M. Sergei Rachmaninoff expressed to me his warm appreciation of its charm and delicate beauty.

Compared with the average concerto this is a short work. It is written in three fairly well-defined sections which are continuous in performance,

'cello Con. Nº 1, Op. 33, in A minor

strikes a mood of vigorous assurance at the outset, and appears throughout the entire concerto. But there is much more thematic material, too extensive to quote from here.

The middle section is sometimes played as an artistic entity, apart from the rest of the composition. It is plaintively appealing, and of altogether exquisite beauty,

cello Con N.º 1. Op 33, in A minor

to the strings of the orchestra, *con sordini*, supply an accompaniment of elusive character that is like the faintly-heard echo of a minuet.

The Second Concerto for violoncello and orchestra, No. 2, Op. 119, in D minor (1902), *is dedicated to M. J. Hollman.*

The Second Concerto for violoncello and orchestra was published in 1903, and is, constructively, a fine work; but one does not find in it the emotional depth, allied to æsthetic beauty, which gives its predecessor high place among the art-creations in the history of the world's music.

Following a structural design of which he frequently made use in his concertos, Saint

H

Saëns has written the Second Concerto for
violoncello in two parts, the movements within
these being continuous.

The concerto opens with an energetic theme,

given out, first, by the orchestra, and then taken
up, solo, by the violoncello.   The mood becomes calmer, and the music is effective for the
cantabile style that can be made extraordinarily
appealing by a good soloist (when he has a good
'cello !).   There are harmonics that stand out
clearly against the slight orchestral background—a mere suggestion of substance, like
the mists that float slowly above marsh-land, on
an autumnal morning.

A *crescendo*, however, brings a re-statement
of the energtic, opening theme, and the intro-
spective mood evaporates—just as the mists do
before the heat of late morning.

In the *Andante sostenuto* that follows, the
mood is meditative—melody for the violoncello
and chords for orchestra that are reflective in
their import.

Part 2 begins *Allegro-non-troppo*, with

bustling energy, and something of defiance. There are conversational passages between soloist and orchestra.

An extended *cadenza*, quasi-recitative, for solo, which is reminiscent of the preceding material, and is like a mental summing-up of an experience, begins what may be regarded as the fourth movement, which is actually concerned with a recapitulation of the principal theme used at the opening of the concerto, but now heard in the key of D major.

PART III

THE SYMPHONIES & SYMPHONIC POEMS

Saint-Saëns wrote—perhaps one should say "completed"—five symphonies, of which only three are published and only one, the Fifth or so-called Third, is much performed.

The First Symphony constituted, as we have seen in Part I. of this book, the master's "arrival" as a composer. In other ways it was important. It brought him closely into touch with Berlioz and Gounod, who were to have an important influence upon his life; it furthered his relationship with the Seghers, through whom he was to meet Mme. Segher's old teacher, Liszt, who influenced his creative art largely, and who was a friend of friends to him; and, what is probably of equal importance in his artistic development, this early success with an important form obviously stimulated the ambitions of the youth. Within the next six years the Second (in F), Third (in D), and Fourth

Symphonies followed fast upon one another, the Third and Fourth being produced in the same year (1859). The Second and Third remain unpublished, so that the Fourth Symphony is usually spoken of as the Second. The "Third" above referred to, was composed much later—in 1886. Its significance, like that of the other two published symphonies, will be considered under its separate analysis.

The First Symphony, in E flat, Op. 2 (1853, published 1855), is dedicated to M. F. Seghers.

There are clear indications of Mozart and Beethoven, in this early work of the youth of seventeen; but it also contains a hint of the mannerisms of the mature genius.

The First Symphony of Saint-Saëns is in four movements. It opens gravely, *Adagio*, but after a few bars a theme—

of a buoyant character is announced on the strings, and appears in various sections of the orchestra, harmonised with Mozartean clarity and grace.

There is another theme of note, first announced by the wood-wind and brass,

which in its confidence of mood, if not in its actual shape, bears affinity to a theme of which considerable use is made in the last movement. The second movement, a *Marche Scherzo*, is exceedingly graceful. Over thin harmonies, *pp.*, on the strings, two oboes give out the theme that is indicative of its dominant mood—

It is so careless, so full of youthful *joie-de-vivre*, so free from the emotional stress with which the music of the composer's middle and later periods is charged, that regarding his art comprehensively one realises the tremendous psychological development which took place. The third movement, an *Adagio*, is more

noteworthy for its advanced harmonic progressions, and the introduction of a harp into the instrumentation—then unusual—than for any marked emotional expression. It is, perhaps, over-long.

Another matter of interest is the merging of the third movement into the fourth, an *Allegro maestoso*, from which a quotation is made above. In addition to the usual assortment of wood-wind, brass, and strings, the ambitious youth has included in the scoring of the Finale of his First Symphony, two saxhorns, three tympani, cymbals, and four harps. Probably this was the part of the composition that particularly provoked the comments of Berlioz and Gounod.

There are full chords for the harps which naturally enriches the orchestral colour.

The mood of the symphony is exuberant throughout, to the point of defiance. It is as though the new composer was conscious of a dawning independence and decided to fling down his gauntlet in the lists of Art.

Apart from the chronological interest, and a certain triteness that occasionally obtrudes, this work impresses one as well worth performance because of its intrinsic beauty. Certainly it ought to be more palatable to present-day audiences than some of the Hadyn still resuscitated.

But then, it would require rehearsal !

*The Second Symphony (Fourth), in A minor,
Op. 55 (1859, published 1878), is dedicated to
M. J. Pasdeloup.*

This symphony opens *Allegro marcato* with
a broad theme of steady rhythm, six crotchets
in the bar—

Second Symphony in A minor, Op.55

Vln 1 *Allegro marcato*

Soon, however, the signature alters to quick
common time, and the mood to *Allegro
appassionato*. The subject of the opening
section appears in an altered melodic guise,
and the rhythm becomes

The music, at first pleading, gradually gains
assurance as the development proceeds on a
classical model, until it attains a condition of
emphatic affirmation, *tutti* and *ff.*, in the concluding seven bars of the movement.

It is as though a wish, half formulated,
became at length definitely realised, and insistently demanded recognition.

The second movement is headed *Adagio,*

and is in three-eight time. It is quite slight and of short duration. The violins, *sordini*, at once announce a theme

Second Symphony in A minor. Op 55

which is artlessly direct in its folksong-like charm. The English horn (solo) makes reply, and then the strings repeat this little song. The orchestration is delicately appropriate.

The mood is quiet, but not sad, and the emotion goes no deeper than a passing regret.

A bright and vivacious *Scherzo Presto* (three-four) takes shape in the third movement. The writing is often polyphonic, and some strident, declamatory passages in double octaves are reminiscent of Beethoven. There is, indeed, nothing very individual about the movement, which might have been written by any well-equipped musician. Nevertheless, it was the part of the symphony that pleased the audience most at a performance, under the direction of the composer, before the Royal Philharmonic Society on 26.3.1898.

The last movement is marked *Prestissimo* (six-eight), and the principal theme, a rippling

melody in quaver triplets which begins on the
last beat of the bar, is ushered in by the violins,
accompanied by the other strings, *pizzicato*.
Soon this melody is doubled by the flutes, and
is, later, harmonised on the rest of the wind and
the strings. The movement, indeed, partakes
of the character of a rondo, of which the
Mozartean theme is the recurring one.

This symphony impresses one more with its
composer's proficiency in technique than with
evidence of outstanding artistic prominence.
As the work of a young man of twenty-three it
is remarkable, as having been done in an age
when the education necessary for the writing of
a musical work of dimensions was more difficult to obtain than it is to-day. The *Adagio*
and *Prestissimo* alone make it worth more
frequent performance.

*The Third Symphony, Op. 78, is in C minor,
and is dedicated to the memory of Franz Liszt*
(1886).

In this splendid symphony one finds a revela-
tion of Saint-Saëns that is uncommon throughout his numerous works, and that is altogether
entrancing.

The symphony is divided into two parts, each
containing two movements which are continuous. A very full orchestra is employed,
including the unusual feature, in scoring for a
symphony, of an organ and two pianofortes.

Merely subordinate use is made of the latter. They are mainly employed in the playing of scales and arpeggi in Part 2; but the organ, which makes its first appearance in the second movement of Part 1, has some very beautiful solo work allotted to it, and belongs integrally to the conceptive idea.

A few impressive chords, *Adagio*, herald the mood of grave questioning that pervades Part 1, even when the prevailing manner, *Allegro moderato*, of the first movement is denoted by an agitated theme, first heard on the strings. The following figure of it appears in an infinite number of modulations throughout the symphony :

Third Symphony in C minor. Op. 78

VlnI&DB

It ebbs and flows, like the voice of conscience, or like materialistic desires, struggling for supremacy over the exaltation of a dawning spiritual serenity. A beautiful theme, announced first on the Cor Anglais, and continued by the wood-wind, appears symbolical of an exalted mood, when heard above the agitated figure on the strings. Eventually it subsides entirely ; but just as surely as humanity

is declared, and divinity is made impossible, by the presence of the Old Adam in us, so do we find the restlessness of this semiquaver figure recurring after an expression of spiritual ecstasy impressively suggested, by several bars in unison, for the whole orchestra.

The entry of the second movement, marked *Poco adagio* (*pp*.), accords with the chastened mood in which the preceding one ends. To obtain an atmosphere suggestive of religious consolation, Saint-Saëns has not relied upon any devices of tonal mimicry, but has employed the very direct means of the organ and four strings (violin 1 and 2, viola, and violoncello). Here is the noble theme, heard on the violins, to which the organ and lower strings supply simple harmony that enhances its grandeur.

Third Symphony in C minor, Op. 78

Vln 1-2

Some delicately-conceived arabesques for the strings, supported by solemn chords on the organ, suggest a state of care-freedom. A figure from the previous movement, reminiscent of earthly desires, appears on the double basses, to be taken up, *crescendo*, by the upper strings. A mystical effect is secured by the employment

of the peculiar tonal qualities of the organ and wind, in an unprepared modulation, before the organ swells forth in a broadly-grand manner, and the movement concludes quietly.

Part 2 begins *Allegro moderato*, and *f.*, and is also ushered in by the strings in agitated fashion, against sustained chords for wood-wind and brass with a figure which may be regarded as a rhythmic variant of that at the beginning of Part 1. The mood of expectancy is maintained, and the indication changes to *Presto*. The music becomes buoyantly exuberant. There is, perhaps consistently enough, a theme, the rhythm and outline of which (in bars of two-four),

Third Symphony in C minor. Op. 78

indicated by this brief quotation, suggest soaring. The subject-matter, both of the *Allegro moderato* and *Presto*, is repeated before a short and quieter section, *Allegro moderato*, in the style of an Intermezzo, and fashioned from yet another variant of the opening theme of Part 1, is reached, and before the fourth movement, *Maestoso*, begins, with a full chord, *f.*, of the tonic major, for organ,

and a grandiose subject, in alternating bars of six-four and nine-four, *tutti*.

The two pianos are busied with arpeggi in groups of semiquaver sextolets, *p.*, providing (with slight support in sustained chords on the organ) a tonal background of delicate beauty for the "conscience" theme, broadly harmonised, and played by the whole of the strings, *divisi*.

It is as if we gazed upon a profile of the Christ, in bas-relief of snowy marble, standing out, emblematic of truth and hope, from a shimmering base of silver and purple.

Around this subject the music gains in significant triumph. Variations of time signature are frequent. Among the most remarkable may be cited those of three-one and three-two, which are perfectly inevitable interpolations in the (usually) steady rhythm of 12 and 6 crotchets in the bar, and are of considerable importance in urging onwards the feeling of majestic grandeur that leads to the climax of the Finale, where organ and orchestra, in a richly-hued wave of sound, express the very definite attainment of rest at a journey's end.

This sublime work may, conceivably, be cherished by posterity along with the other treasures of musical art that are a common heritage of all humanity.

The *Symphonic Poems*, four in number, date from 1871-77. The last, "La Jeunesse

d'Hercule," was thus finished nine years before the death of Liszt, whose genius, in evolving this form (foreshadowed by Beethoven in his Ninth Symphony), Saint-Saëns desired to establish in perpetuity.

While he considerably widened the scope of the form in his Second, Third, and Fourth Poems, it is questionable if his work, fine although it is in many respects, will prove to be more than a stage in an evolutionary process that will take definite shape in yet another form. A dozen years later, Richard Strauss, in the third of his nine contributions to the same form, "Tod und Verklärung," carried the development still further. There is a biology of the Arts as well as of the Sciences.

The earliest of the *Symphonic Poems*, "*Le Rouet d'Omphale*," *Op.* 31 (1871, *published* 1872), is dedicated to Mdlle. Augusta Holmès —that meteoric creature of Irish birth and French adoption, who wrote a little music of imperishable beauty and much of tawdry gilt that has tarnished to verdigris ages since; and whose admirable contempt for the conventions in her feminine impersonation of Don Juan was at one period the amusement of Paris and the horrified scandal of our grandmothers.

Saint-Saëns, to a certain extent, came under the influence of this extraordinary woman, but it is a little unbelievable that he could have regarded her as more than an "episode."

Bearing in mind his ability for judging matters, in a detached way, from *affaires* of the heart to computations of art-worth, the programme of the Poème may be regarded as satirical. At any rate the dedication is peculiarly appropriate.

The composer expresses his conception of the legend of Hercules at the feet of Omphale; and, in the broader sense, the allurement of sexual attraction.

In his prefatory note, he states that the opening figure,

Le Rouet d'Omphale. Op. 31

(indicative of the whirr of the spinning wheel) is chosen only for rhythm, and to give character to the work. This figure persists, with but scant interruption, throughout the entire poem.

It is heard at the commencement, in the *Andantino*, from the first violins (*con sordini*) and then on the flutes (*pp.*), in alternate bars. This scoring, combined with the abrupt change of key which also occurs, produces a peculiarly celestial impression—a sense of a vast space in which is heard musical sounds of ethereal delicacy; a feeling of something altogether remote from the earth.

After some preludial material of this description, of gradually swelling tone-volume, the rhythm of the Omphale *motif* is announced by the wind. The melody of the *motif* is first heard on flutes and violins. The time-signature is six-eight, and the odd rhythm

accentuates the piquant allurement suggested by the chromatic progress of the melody. Thus, indeed, might Eve have beckoned to Adam when he first beheld her in the Garden.

At any rate, Omphale beckons to very considerable purpose. She becomes a little tearful, and then whirrs her spinning wheel and resumes her song, infusing into it greater intensity and a new significance. The orchestral colour is pervaded by this song, and we hear a premonitory sound of the Hercules *motif*.

This is a theme of nobly expressive character, and after a considerable struggle for supremacy it triumphs. The emotional stress subsides, and we have a resumption (but *Allegro*) of the opening mood. The Omphale theme, now in the guise of a *Scherzando*, mocks the fall of the hero. The sounds trail gradually away into silence—the desolation of a heart deceived and made light of—and, like a ghostly memory is heard the whirring of the wheel and the thin,

almost inaudible sound of a harmonic A on the first violins.

The harp is freely employed, and contributes to much of the suggestion of feminine yielding, and grace. There is a pretty continuous background of orchestral colour, and the harmonisation is often thick.

" Le Rouet d'Omphale " is a popular work, although much less so than the third of the Poems, the " Danse Macabre "; but it cannot be regarded as being on its author's highest plane.   The technical resource is admirable, clever; but the sentiment is usually replaced by sentimentality. On occasion I have found it boring.

The Second Symphonic Poem, " Phaéton," Op. 39 (1873, published 1875), is dedicated to Madame Berthe Pochet, née de Tinan.

The prefatory note by the composer to this work informs us that it is concerned with the mythological story of Phaéton's wild ride through the sky, in the chariot of his father, the Sun (Zeus). The rash youth loses control of the steeds, and the flaming chariot approaches the earth.   Disaster threatens the globe, but Jupiter hurls a thunderbolt at the charioteer and thus prevents the impact of the chariot with the earth.

The Poème begins, *Maestoso*, and *f.*, with an impressive chord for the brass and ascending

passages for strings, and then for wood-wind, in demi-semiquavers, terminating in a full chord of the tonic, *tutti*.

Harps, which are freely employed throughout, supported by the strings, then announce a figure,

Allegro animato, which, in one section or other of the orchestra, permeates practically the entire work.

This theme is rhythmically suggestive of the impatient pawing of the steeds, anxious to be off; and later, as it undergoes changes of both accent and key, of their galloping career.

One envisages the gorgeous scene. The handsome, imperious youth, glowing with pride of responsibility and the prospect of his adventurous journey through limitless space, and barely able to control his team. Around him the glory of the Sun, and the faint blue of the dim distance broken by fleecy, white clouds.

A noble theme, on the horns, appears to symbolise the farewell advice of his father, Zeus.

Phaéton traverses space. There is a certain

sense of assurance, and defiance, in the new theme heard, *f.* and *marcato* on trumpets and trombones in unison, and then taken up, *ff.*, by the wood-wind.

The charioteer rushes onwards at a headlong pace.   Harps, *divisi*, in arpeggi, and richly-coloured chords add their quota of movement to the agitated re-iteration of the rhythmic opening theme on wood-wind and strings. The music increases in animation, then the second theme of Phaéton is given to both wood-wind and brass to an accompaniment of agitated quaver triplets on the strings.

A new theme, of a reflective, pastoral type, may symbolise the youth's dreams of future power.   He becomes heedless of the wildly erratic pounding of the hoofs in front of him, but their sound grows in insistence and forces attention.   He attempts, unsuccessfully, to regain control.

The tumult increases, and culminates in a blare of sound from the entire orchestra, *fff.* Jupiter hurls the thunderbolt!   The fateful race is finished.

One hears the voice of Zeus again, sorrowfully mourning; and there is an agonised version of poor Phaéton's once triumphant theme, ere the poem end.

"Phaéton" is a very beautiful composition, delicately sensitive in colour suggestion by reason of the skilful instrumentation and the

clever juxtaposition of the major and minor modes which, even at the outset, gives to the music an eerie feeling of ominous dread : a kind of premonition of impending disaster.

The Third Symphonic Poem, " *Danse Macabre*," *Op.* 40 (1874, *published* 1875), is almost the best known to the general public of all the master's works. By the "general public " one means, of course, that section of the public that does not, ordinarily, attend concerts of good music, or West End recitals; but that hears its music *via* the café orchestra, the en'tracte in the theatre or music hall, and the cinema. By the same channels this public knows the name of Saint-Saëns as the composer of " Softly Awakes my Heart," although they have probably never heard of " Samson et Dalila"; and of " The Swan," although if reference was made to " Le Cygne " and " Le Carnaval des animaux," from which it is the sole published number, they would be equally uninformed.

The "Danse Macabre" was suggested by some verses of Henri Cazalis, and, briefly, is concerned with a spectral waltz danced in a graveyard by skeletons, which behave in a thoroughly conventional manner by commencing their revels after the clock has struck the hour of midnight, and then decorously returning to their tombs at cock-crow.

There is nothing at all original in the

scoring, although the composer has succeeded realistically in translating the grisly and unpleasant idea of the verses into terms of music.

The twelve strokes of the witching hour are sounded by horn and harp, and muted violins are used in the time-honoured "mystical" manner. And then we have the only really original idea in the whole Poem—the tuning of the E string of the solo violin, that gives out the melody of the waltz, half a tone lower. The clattering bones are obviously imitated on the xylophone, and cock-crow is imitated on the oboe. "Tricks" (as Saint-Saëns would probably have agreed himself) "that every well-equipped musician has up his sleeve."

Probably the cheapness of the effects in this work is responsible for the light regard in which one sometimes finds the works of the master held by serious musicians who are probably only acquainted with his compositions of "popular" genre.

The Fourth, and last, of the Symphonic Poems, "La Jeunesse d'Hercule," Op. 50 (1877, published 1877), dedicated to Mr. Henri Duparc, has the following literary preface affixed to it by Saint-Saëns :—

"The fable relates that at the beginning of his life Hercules saw two roads opening before him; that of pleasure and that of virtue. Insensible to the allurements of the nymphs and bacchantes, the hero enters the path

of strife and combat, at the end of which he discerns, through the flames of the stake, the recompense of immortality.''

"La Jeunesse d'Hercule" has a theme of striving, and assertive, character as its *leit-motif*. This theme may be regarded as emblematic of the hero's personality.

Soon, on the wood-wind, and later with harp support, is heard a little theme, *espressivo*, in nine-eight, which has an airy grace, and a rhythm that is fancifully suggestive of beckoning hands. The suggestion of this theme is undoubtedly allurement. Even thus early in his progress, the hero encounters the nymphs, and bacchantes.

A dance figure, *Allegro* (quick common time), in the rhythm of which there is a hint of barbaric abandon, is used in working up to a mood of revelry before the return of the broadly-noble Hercules *motif*, *ff.*, seems to indicate an effort of the hero to cast aside the wiles of his temptresses.

This is followed by an *Andante sostenuto*, in which the *motif* grows more insistent, and the scoring is grandiose in style. A re-appearance of the nymphs' theme—now in crotchet triplets to the bar of common time—perhaps indicates that temporary surrender to the animal passions may influence the growth of spiritual perfection.

The finale is a *Maestoso* of short duration.

Great use is made in it of agitated sequential groups of demi-semiquavers to create the impression of the triumphant hypothesis of Hercules.

"La Jeunesse d'Hercule" is a sensitive appreciation of the literary text, united to fine constructive ability. The poetical conception is lower, however, than that of "Phaéton."

PART III

CHAMBER MUSIC

Saint-Saëns has left over a dozen works which belong to the category of Chamber music, and particulars of them will be found in the Appendix.

His work in this peculiarly exacting realm of composition is eloquent of his sound musicianship and the clearness of his part-writing. Often, too, is present, in the emotional expression, an intimate sense of naïveté as unspoilt as that of a light-hearted, lovable child.

In the year in which his first symphony was published (1855) he wrote his first chamber work, the *Quintet for pianoforte and strings, Op.* 14, which was published ten years later by J. Hamelle, Paris. It is distinctly classical in feeling and construction, and shows certain mannerisms that became established subsequently. In fact, it shows a logical expansion

of the independent outlook exhibited in the
symphony alluded to, which was, of course,
written two years earlier.

The next composition belonging to the category with which we are now concerned is the
popular *Trio in F, Op.* 18, *for pianoforte, violin
and violoncello* (1863, *published* 1867), *dedicated to Mons. Alfred Lamarche.* The mood
in this trio is one of light-hearted confidence,
the pure happiness of a care-free mind amid
congenial surroundings, rather than the confidence that is born of arrogance, or of the grim
determination to succeed.

A steady rhythm of three-four is established
in the first four bars of the *Allegro vivace*, in
which the work begins, before the violoncello
announces an irresponsible little melody—

Trio in F. Op. 18

'cello

It is repeated by the violin, and then by the
piano, which, at the conclusion of its amplified
version, gives another theme, little more than a
figure, which undergoes considerable development throughout the movement.

The *Andante* is quite short and charmingly
fresh. The piano states the theme, in unisons,
against a sustained octave A on the violin.

Before the end of the duet the viola enters with
a doubling of the melody on the piano, and
then these two busy themselves with a gracious
accompaniment when the violin sings the tune.

There is a contrasted subject—

Trio in F. Op. 18

Vln   *Poco piu mosso quasi Allegretto, tempo rubato*

a flowing melody given entirely to the strings
before a brief repetition of the first subject
brings the movement to an end.

The concluding movement is a *Scherzo*
(Presto) of varied themes and epigrammatic
style. A fragment of the first theme of the
Andante appears, but inconspicuously. A
condition of suppressed excitement is apparent. There is much brilliant writing, particularly for piano, and the Trio concludes em-
phatically, *molto allegro.*

There are two *Quartets for Strings. The
First, Op.* 112, *for* 2 *violins, viola, and violoncello, was composed and published in* 1899, *and
is dedicated to Mons. Eugéne Ysaÿe.*

It contains four movements. The opening
Allegro molto is of serene and happy mood.
The second subject ripples onward with the
careless abandon of a brook in Maytime.
There is a strangely accented theme that

enters somewhat dramatically with a bar of twelve-four, soon altered to six-four, for viola, before the development and recapitulation on the usual lines of sonata form.

The second movement, *Molto allegretto quasi presto*, is a gay rondo.   There is a certain allurement about the theme announced by the first violin,

1ˢᵗ String Quartet. Op. 112

accompanied *pizzicato* by the lower strings, and, in due course, varied to groups of quaver triplets.

The slow movement, *Molto adagio*, is concerned with an aria for violin 1 of a longing, empyrean type, which becomes a little passionate, a little regretful before it concludes.   The movement ends on an harmonic A, for all the parts.

In the final *Allegro non troppo* there is a resumption of the mood of the first movement, and a good deal of clever part-writing, sustaining the interest for all the players before the brilliant ending.

The *Second Quartet for Strings, Op.* 153, for the same combination of instruments as the First (2 *violins, viola, and 'cello*), *was composed*

in 1919, and is therefore an example of the concluding work of the master. It is *dedicated to Mons. Jacques Durand.* The first movement, *Allegro animato*, opens energetically—

2*nd* String Quartet Op. 153

remarkable as an expression of emotion from a man of eighty-four; but after considerable vigour, and variations of rhythm, key and subject-matter, the music evaporates, *pp.*, in a chord of the tonic (G major) for all the instruments.

Two personalities appear to strive for supremacy in the very expressive second movement of this quartet. The figuration indicative of the first, pessimistic and heavy, is labelled *Molto adagio.* Opposed to it is an *Andantino cantabile*, a little vague, a little wondering, but calmer, and more hopeful. These moods alternate throughout. It is as if two dear friends discussed a problem, and the one sought to sustain and encourage the other; but the movement ends in a state of questioning.

The third movement is marked, "*Interlude et Final.*" The Interlude is a serene *Andantino* laid out chiefly for the two lower strings. It is succeeded by an *Allegretto con moto* that

has about it the fresh joyousness of a sunny day
in spring. The following figure, which recurs
frequently in all the parts, is largely responsible for this genial impression :—

2nd String Quartet. Op. 153

Allegretto con moto

Much earlier than the quartets for strings is
the *Quartet in B flat, Op.* 41 (1875), *for pianoforte, violin, viola, and violoncello.* It is a
musicianly work, classical in structure, and
bound together by thematic allusions in the
last movement to subject-matter that occurs in
the first. There is a fine chorale in the *Andante
maestoso,* and, later, an example of the whim-
sical style of writing that one finds in the
Allegro scherzando of the Second Pianoforte
Concerto, and in the " Danse Macabre."
The piano quartet has enjoyed considerable
popularity.

Sonata No. 1, *Op.* 32, *in C minor, for violoncello and pianoforte* (1872, *published* 1873).

The dramatic opening of this impressive
sonata, indeed the emotions expressed during
the whole of the composition, are surely influenced by the trials through which Saint-Saëns
had just passed, from which, in fact, he was
hardly free, at the time of its conception.

1st Sonata. 'cello & piano, in C minor. Op. 32

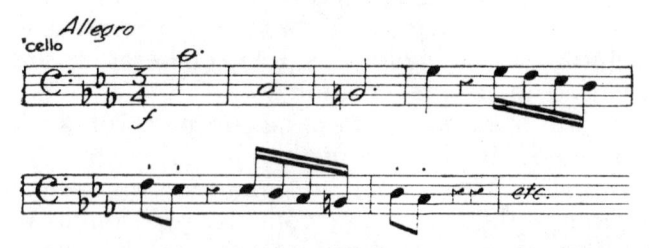

The agonised sobs of these opening bars
remind one of the anguished chords with which
Chopin begins his Sonata in B flat minor,
Op. 35, for pianoforte. The emotion is tur-
bulent, and the pianoforte is busied with rapid
semiquaver passages in scales and arpeggi,
against a broad melody for 'cello.

A period of calm in the tonic major is soon
swept aside in the development section of the
movement, and the mood becomes increasingly
stressful, brief, calm passages, *pp.*, serving but
to increase the poignancy of the emotion.

The second movement, *Andante tranquillo
sostenuto*, consists of a lovely melody—

1st Sonata, 'cello & piano, in C minor. Op. 32

In the pianoforte accompaniment to this the
theme is allied to harmony of chorale-like.
clarity. The melody is then elaborated, and
varied in its presentation.

This *Andante* is an exquisite piece of work,
imbued with a sense of the ineffable calm, that
is half languor, half resignation, which may
come to the solace of emotions overwrought by
a very desolation of grief.

The mood of the last movement, an *Allegro
moderato*, is one of rather passionate defiance,
significant of renewed strength, and courage in
Life's battle. The opening theme,

to which there is an agitated accompaniment,
in semiquavers, for pianoforte, serves as an
index to the emotional condition dominating
it. There is much brilliant writing for both
instruments.

Sonata No. 2, Op. 123, *in F* (1905, *published*
1905), *for violoncello and pianoforte. Dedicated to Mons. Jules Griset.*

The Second Sonata for 'cello and piano is
an elaborate and musicianly brilliant, rather

than an emotionally intense, work. It demands technique of a high grade from both performers, throughout.

In the first movement, *Maestoso largamente,* two individualities are indicated. One is of an energetic, bustling kind, and is denoted chiefly by the following rhythm, in varying melodic figures—

while the other is playfully flippant—

2nd Sonata, 'cello & piano, in F Op. 123

A beautiful theme introduces an element of serenity into the duologue. The development of the material is on classical lines.

The second movement, headed *Scherzo con variazioni,* and beginning *Allegro animato,* is a really fine example of the variation style of writing. The statement of the bustling theme is made by the piano in unison octaves. Of this there are eight variations, pleasantly contrasted in rhythm and mood.

A " Romanza," *Poco adagio e molto espressivo,* with melodiously grateful writing for the

K

'cello, sustained mostly by an accompaniment of broken chords and arpeggi on the piano, occupies the third movement.

The last movement, *Allegro non troppo grazioso*, is indeed of a gracious and flowing character. It is like the harmonious conclusion of a conversation, begun in some dissent, and made tender and amiable by reminiscences of past happiness.

There is a delightful little *cantabile* theme of which much use is made.

PART III

Theme IV

VARIAZIONI

To discuss in detail the very large miscellaneous output of Saint-Saëns is quite beyond the space of the present work. If one considered the many songs and small pieces for instrumental solo and duet seriatim, in a larger book even, no really useful purpose would be served, for they belong to the class of music that is most likely to be already in possession of the musically-interested reader.

There are, however, several fine and important works of dimensions that belong to none of the usual forms already considered, and that I have therefore decided to regard collectively under the above heading.

Foremost of these compositions must be placed the beautiful *Fantaisie for pianoforte and orchestra, Op.* 89 (1891), to which the composer gave the title of "*Africa.*" There is no dedication, a rather unusual circumstance for an important work of the master's.

The Fantaisie is, constructively, a tone-poem

for pianoforte and orchestra.   The music is,
frankly, programmatic, but it is programme
music that attempts, and with conspicuous
success, to conjure, by means of aural suggestion, a vision that is almost tangible in the
intensity of its appeal to the emotions.

Listening to the reedy little air—

that issues, first from the oboes and then from
the flutes, above a steady rhythm of six-eight
in the strings of the *Molto allegro*, one might
be the unsuspected hearer of the commencement of the native music ushering in a night of
religious dance revels in an African village.

Increasing animation is imparted to the
music by the entrance of the solo instrument
with the theme in bold, double octaves, while
the strings maintain their re-iteration of the
quaver figure and the higher wood-wind sounds
tied chords.   The instrumentation further suggests the tum-tum sounds elicited by the fingers
of negro musicians from gourd and skin drums,
and the soft movement of the cool evening
breeze.

The frenzy of the dancers increases.   More
worshippers at the shrine of the god who
happens to be the object of the ritual become

possessed by the divine afflatus and sway
uncertainly. The accent of the music is erratic,
from the normal to a stress on the first, third,
and sixth beats in the bar.

Brilliant scale passages for the pianoforte
lead to an *Andante espressivo* in three-four
that might be a fragment of a folk song. Calm
succeeds the emotional stress, like the peaceful
glow of a cool evening after a thundery day.

This mood does not endure for long, however. Soon, *pp.*, returns the monotonous
imitative drum taps, on the strings, and the
dance re-commences.

Fragments of melody, like the sighs and
murmurs of lovers in the glamour of the per-
fumed night, appear and disappear in the
general hubbub and blare of tonal colour which
eddies around the principal theme alluded to,
and for a considerable time the music pursues
its course, *ff.*, to a brilliant termination. The
revellers have abandoned themselves to the
spell of the African night, and will dance until
they sink to the ground in a stupor of
exhaustion.

"Africa" is in the freest Fantasia form. It
gives plenty of scope for technical display, including sound production, and is very popular
alike with artists and public.

Two other works, for pianoforte and orchestra, which are popular as concert pieces, are
the *Allegro appassionato, Op.* 70, and the

Rhapsodie d'Auvergne, Op. 73. Both belong to the year 1884.

The former is a graceful composition, *Allegro, Andantino,* and *Allegro,* in which the pianoforte is employed with the thematic material and its elaborations, in the first and last sections, and the orchestra provides, in the middle part, a brief period of reposeful contrast. The *Allegro appassionato* is a favourite with concert pianists, but is of no great importance.

There are several compositions for violin and orchestra, notably the *Introduction et Rondo Capriccioso* (1863, *published* 1870), *Op.* 28; the "*Havanaise*" (1887, *published* 1888), *Op.* 83, a brilliant work very familiar to concert-goers; and the *Caprice Andalous* (1904), *Op.* 122.

The *Introduction et Rondo Capriccioso* referred to above is dedicated, like so much of Saint-Saëns' music for the violin, to the late Señor P. Sarasate. The *Andante malinconico* (two-four) opens with a questioning theme for the solo violin. This theme is somewhat amplified before a brilliant arpeggio passage, terminating in a couple of bars of trilling, leads to the *Allegro ma non troppo* (six-eight) at the middle of the fourth bar of which the soloist announces the theme of the Rondo. It is of a delicately fresh character, essentially violinistic in its halting rhythm, and is duly

succeeded by a second theme of more tranquil mood.

After both, and especially the initial theme, have passed through various rhythmic and modulatory metamorphosis, and have afforded the violinist opportunity for the display of all manner of technical fireworks, including some effective double-stopping, the brief *Piu allegro* is reached. Here the solo instrument is engaged, from start to finish, in a display of scale and arpeggio playing which rushes onwards until the fourth last bar, and ends in a blare of sound for the whole orchestra. The work is exceedingly popular as a show piece.

Marche Héroïque, Op. 34, *for orchestra, dedicated to the memory of Henri Regnault* (1871, *published* 1871). Composed, as related in Part I. of this book, to the memory of a dearly-loved friend of Saint-Saëns, who was killed during the siege of Paris in 1870.

This march is mainly vigorous, and optimistic in mood. Save in the rhythm of the introductory matter to the last section it is not of the customary "Marche militaire" type.

The central *Andantino* is tenderly expressive of deep sorrow. A beautiful figure in three-four is given to the violins, *pp.*, with a solo theme for trombones and colourful harmony for harp and wood-wind.

Undoubtedly the charming "*Suite Algerienne,*" *Op.* 60 (1880, *published* 1881), is among

the most popular of the orchestral works of lighter genre left to us by the master. The suite contains four numbers which are sometimes performed as separate items.

No. 1, *Prélude.* (A street in Algiers.) *Molto allegro* (six-eight).

The music begins, *pp.*, with a roll on the tympani, which, by the way, continues to rumble, in muffled sounds, for about fifty bars. A fragment of a theme is heard, soon, on the violoncellos. Later, it is amplified, and transformed to use as a little air—of reedy, Oriental *timbre*, such as a Moorish street musician might tootle on his early morning perigrinations. Animation arises gradually, in the tone picture presented, until an arresting figure, oddly harmonised in fifths and thirds, reminds one of the *gendarmes.* Largely by the employment of unison passages, and flowing arpeggi, the composer preserves the thinness and monotony of colour that is conventionally Moorish.

The street we are asked to imagine is a busy place of life and movement. Apparently it is in the picturesque native quarters, and has nothing to do with the modernised French localities of the city. Perhaps one ought to substitute "little" for "nothing," for as the music subsides into silence we hear, in the distance, a little bugle call, unmistakably martial, that must surely issue from a barracks.

No. 2, " *Rhapsodie Mauresque.*" The second number of the suite is marked *Allegretto non troppo*. It undergoes frequent changes of time signature and rhythm, and constitutes an excellent example of exotic assimilation. Not for a moment, as in the first number, are we permitted to think of other surroundings than those implied by the title.

The melodic material, plentiful enough, is mostly in the shape of fragmentary little figures —one can hardly term them themes—reminiscent, either of a reed instrument voiced by wind, from a goat-skin, or the mouth of the player.

Cymbals, triangle, and tympani, are freely used towards the close, and a sense of cross-rhythm (two-four against three-four) is established in a dance measure which brings the Rhapsodie to a clangous, and scintillating, conclusion.

No. 3, " *Rèverie du Soir,*" is marked *Allegretto quasi Andantino* (six-eight), and is short and reposeful. Scraps of melody, chiefly on the wood-wind, are vaguely reminiscent of the scenes conjured by the two preceding numbers of the suite. The strings are employed in a manner imitative of the twanging of a guitar.

No. 4, "*Marche Militaire Française.*" *Allegro giocoso* (quick common time).

A vigorous, military march about which little

need be said. The thematic material is tuneful, and the orchestration highly decorative—

Suite Algerienne Nº 4, Op. 60

But although a piece of this description is conceivably an actuality in a picture of Algiers, the impression jars, and one feels that the suite would have benefited, poetically, without the addition of this number; or else by the substitution for it of a less blatant composition.

An examination of the list of compositions for piano solo written by Saint-Saëns reveals the surprising fact that there is not even one Sonata among them. For very many years, as everybody knows, the sonatas of Mozart and then of Beethoven, held sway in this particular musical form—their influence is still strong—and it is feasible to think that Saint-Saëns very possibly, in his earlier years at all events, did not wish to be classified with the lesser composers of the period who turned out sonatas and sonatinas for the use of girls' seminaries. Since, however, Chopin and Schumann had but recently made notable contributions to that class of pianoforte literature, and Liszt (who, both as a composer and a man, the young man was wont to regard as a model) indicates new

possibilities in his Sonata in B minor, it is, I
repeat, surprising, to the point of amazement,
that no Sonata for piano alone is published.
Among the scribblings of his childhood he
hints that such a composition existed, but we
know that he destroyed many of these fruits of
immaturity. But many early overtures, cantatas, and so forth went the same way, so that
the circumstance is no explanation of his
neglect of the form in his maturity.

Some of his numerous transcriptions for
piano are almost as popular with pianists
as his few original works of importance.
Examples of this kind that one involuntarily
recalls are the transcription of the Chorus of
Dervishes from Beethoven's " The Ruins of
Athens," the " Caprice sur les airs de ballet
d'Alceste" of Gluck, and the transcription of
the Scherzo from Mendelssohn's immortal
overture to · " A Midsummer Night's Dream."

However, his Opus 3 (Op. 2 is the first
symphony) is devoted to six bagatelles for
piano (1855, published 1856), and there are
two books of six Etudes (Op. 52, 1877, and
Op. 111, 1899), which are notable, and useful,
contributions to the library of the pianist.
Most concert-goers have heard the " Etude en
forme de valse " and the " Etude de rythme."

Duets, written for one and for two pianos
(four hands), received considerable attention.
The " Variations sur un thème de Beethoven "

(*i.e.*, the Trio of the minuet in the Sonata of Beethoven, Op. 31) (1874), and the fine "Scherzo" for two pianos, Op. 87 (1889, published 1890), alluded to in Part I. of this book, are representative of this sphere of productivity.

The songs, numerically, far exceed in importance all the other compositions for instrumental solo. The beautiful "Mélodies Persanes," sung first by the composer's friend Henri Regnault; "Pourquoi rester seulette," "Danse Macabre," "Extase," "Désir de l'Orient"—in such as these the vocalist, who is also an artist, is well served. There are also a number of vocal duets.

The vocal scena, or ballade, for mezzo-soprano and orchestra, " La Fiancée du Timbalier " (1887, Op. 82), to the words of Victor Hugo, and the "Air du Rossignol" from the incidental music which Saint-Saens wrote to Mme. Jane Dieulafoy's drama "Parysatis" (1902) are both favourites with the more ambitious of our women vocalists.

The works which the master wrote specially for the organ have been somewhat overshadowed in popularity with soloists on that instrument by transcriptions from his operatic and orchestral works. The attention of organists may be directed to the two books of Three Preludes and Fugues (1894, Op. 99, and 1898,

Op. 109), and to the later of the four Fantaisies enumerated in the Appendix.

The fact that three of the last compositions given Opus numbers, *i.e.*, "Cyprès et Lauriers," Fantaisie Op. 157, and "Prière," are concerned with the organ is indicative of an abiding affection for that really noble, but much abused, instrument.

PART III

THEME V

WORKS FOR THE STAGE

Early environment, associates of student days, and inherent fondness for the theatre and for the rôle of *mime*, in private amusements, are all circumstances that make the predilection of Saint-Saëns for expression, *via* Opera, easily understandable.

His mother's friends, the Garcia sisters (Mme. Malibran and Mme. Pauline Viardot), and the circle in which they moved; Gounod, Rossini, Auber—all his seniors, all devoted friends of his, and all, as everybody knows, conspicuously successful in their time as composers of operatic music; his most intimate fellow-students and contemporaries at the Conservatoire—Bizet, whose success at a period that was peculiarly difficult for young composers who desired to shine in opera, was encouraging; Massenet, whose popularity was even more level; Delibes, whose ambitions, like those of the young Saint-Saëns, lay opera-wards—all spoke and thought of opera, all

regarded success in that art-form as their Elysium.

What has this influence produced in the form of opera?

Baldly speaking, some thirteen works, one of which is not entirely the work of Saint-Saëns; and of these thirteen, only one, "Samson et Dalila," has achieved permanent favour with the public.

The success of this one work has, however, been tremendous, and has gained for the master, solely on account of its creation, lasting recognition as a composer of grand opera.

The success of "Samson et Dalila" has overshadowed all later and earlier works. Addressed casually regarding Saint-Saëns' operas, ordinarily well-informed fellow-musicians are prone to reply, "Yes! Delightful work, ' Samson and Delilah,' isn't *it*?" or, " Oh! I can't stand ' Samson and Delilah!' Too much . . . ." according to the breadth, or narrowness, of the speaker's outlook. But never a word about any of the other twelve brethren!

Saint-Saëns was not well served in the matter of plot and libretto for the majority of his operas. This was, for him, peculiarly unfortunate. His sensitiveness to extraneous suggestion, to anything in the nature of a programme, which explains the appeal of his instrumental programme music (and of

"Samson" for that matter), prevented him
from ignoring his libretto as other composers,
whose talents lay in the creation of absolute
music, have done when saddled with a stupid
or badly-constructed libretto.   What, for example, would Saint-Saëns have made of the
insipidity of the libretto in "Il Seraglio" or
"Il Flauto Magico"?   Or Mozart of the intensity of the situations that arise in "Samson"
and "Henry VIII."?   I make the grotesque
suggestion to illustrate my thesis that the
emotional make-up and inherent common-
sense of the Frenchman made it impossible
for him to accept the wild improbabilities and
utterly artificial state of affairs in the conventional operatic story.

This is shown in the "plot" of the first
opera "*Le Timbre d'Argent*," the libretto of
which, by Michel Carré and Jules Barbier, was
given to the composer, at the request of Auber,
by Carvalho, the director of the Théâtre-
Lyrique.   Several other musicians had refused
it!

The story is, briefly, a re-hash of Faust, but
—and here lies probably the explanation of
the failure of the opera—the fantasy is not
courageously maintained.   Evidently its wild
improbability was too much even for the
authors, or the composer (who has recorded
that he had alterations made in the libretto), for
any dramatic strength it possesses is negatived,

at the end, by the explanation that the whole thing is but a dream!

The devil takes the name, and character, of Doctor Spiridion. The hero is a young painter, Conrad, who is engaged to a beautiful, and good, woman, Hélène, but who is attracted, indeed, fascinated, by the allurements of a dancer, Fiametta. Now, the dancer, like many of her profession, loves the good things of life, and Conrad craves a plentiful supply of lucre in order to gratify his desires of the moment.

This is an apportunity really too good for the devil to miss! He presents Conrad with a magical bell that will grant his need of gold when it is rung, but that will at the same time cause someone near to him to fall down dead.

Conrad, a very commonplace kind of an Adam, goes on ruthlessly, after the manner of his kind, until one day the victim of the spell, by means of which he is able to live his riotous life, chances to be his friend, Benedict. Between the horror of this, and his still slumbering love for Hélène, he breaks the bell, and the spell, and—awakens!

The music is not very interesting, and unequal. But considering the many alterations which the opera underwent, before its production on February 23rd, 1877, under a subsidy from the Ministry of Fine Arts, at the (then) bankrupt Lyrique, this fact is not remarkable.

L

Poor Saint-Saëns could not induce Carvalho to listen to the music for two years after his feverish writing of it!

Carvalho, and his wife, when they eventually heard it, liked it at once; but the impresario, like some theatrical managers of to-day had more than a weakness for "arrangements" and "collaborations"—particularly mean forms of vandalism when forced upon impecunious creative artists—and so, more delay. Then came the failure of the Lyrique.

At the Opera was a director of similar ambitions. He wanted a burlesque part for a favourite of his; in fact, the opera was to be cut about again to suit the lady who was really much more important than a work of art! Deadlock, once more!!

After that, a dancer who proved to be only a *mime*; a tenor who, for no sane reason, threw up his rôle; the war of 1870 and divers other worries all occurred to delay production until 1877. Really, the pre-natal history of this opera is more absorbing than the plot of the opera itself!

It was repeated at Brussels two years later, and again in 1907 at Monte Carlo. But neither these, nor later revivals, have been enduringly successful.

The overture is worth concert performance, and one of the airs, "Le Bonheur est chose légère," was heard quite recently in London

with violin *obbligato*. Bizet prepared the piano and vocal score.

The efforts of Saint-Saëns to secure performance of "Le Timbre d'Argent" brought him into touch with du Locle, who, to fill in time while they waited for a dancer, introduced him to Gallet and suggested that they should co-operate in "*La Princesse Jaune*," a little one-act piece with which Saint-Saëns made his début on the stage on June 12th, 1872.

There is some uncertainly about the year. The composer himself, in his "École Buissonière," is contradictory. He says that he was thirty-five when this little opera was produced. That would mean that it was performed during the unrest of the summer of 1870 that preceded the national tragedy of the autumn—which is hardly likely. And, further, he says that it was in 1871 that he first met Gallet over this very matter of collaboration. We may, therefore, accept the year given as being most likely correct, which means, of course, that the composer was almost thirty-seven at the time of his operatic début.

Japan was a European craze of the period. The two artists were all for a purely Japanese creation—naturally. To this, du Locle demurred. The compromise was therefore adopted of making a young Dutch scientist conceive an infatuation for a Japanese statuette, and under the influence of a drug, fancy

himself in Japan. On awakening from the "sleep" he finds his cousin, who loves him, by his side.

The piece is a fragile fancy to which the composer wrote charming music. The score bears evidence of his *penchant* for oriental colour, and happy knack of suggesting it.

The work has had successful revivals in France, and might be heard here advantageously.

While "Le Timbre d'Argent" was pursuing its uncertain course towards production, the composer was writing his happy "hit"— "*Samson et Dalila*," first simply styled "Dalila" and then "Samson," and produced, through the instrumentality of Liszt, at the *Grand Ducal Theatre of Weimar on December 2nd*, 1877.

Saint-Saëns has freely acknowledged that without the help and influence of Liszt, who, although he had not heard a note of the opera, engaged him to finish it and produce it at Weimar, "Samson" would probably never have seen the light.

The composer had already given a private performance of the second act at his house, when Regnault was the "Samson." His friends thought he must he mad to attempt a Biblical subject. No manager would listen to him. Here, in England, we went one better in broad-mindedness and refused to sanction

its performance, on the stage until 1909. In France they were a little better. They heard it in 1890, first at Rouen and then in Paris, after its triumphs all around had, figuratively, shamed them into hearing it. Lacking moral courage we sanctioned its performance, *as an oratorio*, at a concert at Covent Garden, in 1893, under Sir Frederic Cowen.

Without attempting to pry into the minds of those individuals who fondly believe that their own particular little latch-key is the only one that will cause the gates of Heaven to swing back—since this book is concerned with the life and art of a genius, and not with theology—I will pass on from this phase of the opera's production and consider the familiar material of which it is made up.

The plot, around which Ferdinand Lemaire has written his libretto, adheres to the Biblical story. The appeal is human, natural, and thoroughly straightforward. It is of long ago, it is of to-day, it is for all time, for it is of human love and passion, and its betrayal—and who does not imagine himself, or herself, in either of the title-rôles? And for those who do not apprehend these things there is spectacle in gorgeous profusion.

There is no overture. The construction of the musical edifice is cemented together by the recurrence of thematic material. The acts are divided into scenes, which was an innovation,

like the absence of overture, at the time the opera was written.

The curtain rises with the commencement of the grave music, and the sound of the voices of the children of Israel bemoaning their captivity, first heard from behind the curtain. Music for chorus is usually either dull or rowdy in effect. In this case dullness is avoided in the nick of time by the dramatic arrival of Samson, and the episode between him and Abimelech. Shouting their revolt the crowd rush from the stage and the high priest of Dagon enters and discovers the insurrection.

At this juncture a group of Hebrew patriarchs chant an ancient psalm in praise of the deliverance of their race. If this is well sung it is effective; but that is, unfortunately, seldom the case, and so the audience often experiences a very dull patch before the arrival of Delilah, with her maidens, and her garlands of flowers, appears, and begins her allurement of the strong man. An old Hebrew acts the rôle of conscience, and wise counsel, and attempts to stem the current of the swiftly-growing fascination that increases in its devastating effect upon Samson.

The voluptuous appeal of the music, melodious, rhythmically compelling, and subtly challenging in its suggestion of pent-up passion, proves irresistible. The high priestess of Dagon gains a moral victory as her maidens

dance entrancingly and she sings her famous song of Spring.

The action of the second act takes place outside the house of Delilah, at nightfall, in the valley of Sorek. Saint-Saëns got his idea for the tempest which rumbles through this act from the tempest in the last act of Rossini's "Othello."

The ominous atmosphere of this sullen mood of Nature provides an appropriate background for the intrigues of Delilah and the High Priest, who plot the downfall of Samson; and later renders almost sinister her feigned outburst of passionate entreaty in the melody, best known of all as an except from the opera, "Mon cœur s'ouvre à ta voix."

Still Samson vacillates before the enchantress. Then, goaded to action by her behaviour as she rushes into the house, he follows her, and is shorn of his glory and his strength.

A great deal depends here upon how the shorn locks are exhibited. If they are held aloft, as sometimes happens, it is almost impossible to repress one's merriment. The thing savours of farce. But that can quite easily be avoided by showing them—when such a course is adopted—in a derisive, instead of in a triumphant, fashion.

Act III. contains a tableau and a fine, spectacular scene, and is thus planned with thought for the exigencies of staging.

The tableau shows the blinded and shorn
hero turning the grinding-mill. To Heaven
he appeals in anguished manner for mercy, and
the voices of his fellow Israelites are heard,
accusing him of having failed them.

The final scene is a very splendid one, and
shows the interior of the temple of Dagon. The
sacred fire is burning a bluish flame. They
frequently contrive to make it ascend and
descend to the rhythm of the music, a rather
flamboyant canon in the singing of which the
high priest and Delilah lead.

Samson makes his appearance in this scene,
led in by a little boy. Delilah, with true vixen-
ish enjoyment, taunts him, with his subjection,
by singing fragments of the love-motifs from
the seduction phase of the enslavement.
Samson is then led away.

There is a sparkling ballet to exquisite music
of the Eastern colour so beloved by the master.
This item, like the famous song, and the dance
of the priestesses already alluded to, is very
often heard as a separate item at concerts, in
cafés, played by seaside bands; in fact, everywhere, expected and unexpected. It is founded
on a genuine Oriental theme given to the composer by General Yusuf.

Samson, in a powerful voice, standing between massive pillars at the back of the stage,
appeals to Heaven for strength if only for a
moment, to annihilate his enemies. The struc-

ture falls and all are buried beneath its ruins—
at least such is the effect at the abrupt, and most
dramatic, conclusion of the opera.

*Étienne Marcel, an opera in four acts, words
by Louis Gallet, was first produced at Lyons
on February 8th, 1879.*

It suffers from a conventional "happy"
ending, atop of distinctly tragic incident.

The plot is, briefly, concerned with insurrection in Paris in the year 1358, when, under the
regency of the Dauphin Charles, Étienne
Marcel, a provost of the merchant classes,
planned a revolt against the regent, lost his
popularity with the mob, played traitor, and
opened the gates of the city to Charles of
Navarre.

The love interest centres around his
daughter, Beatrice, and an equerry to the
Dauphin, Robert de Lorris.

Marcel is assassinated, for his treachery, and
his daughter throws herself, tragically, upon his
body.   Her lover tries to induce her to flee with
him.

At this stage, by all the unwritten laws of
opera, the lovers should die or be killed, together; or "curtain" might have been arranged
for in some manner less harrowing to the feel-
ings of the tender-hearted.

Instead, we have a flourish of trumpets,
heralding the entry of the Dauphin, and the
opera ends vociferously.

The music is pleasing, and adequate. The
composer finds most scope for his fertile
imagination in the scenes of riot and disorder.
There is some delightful ballet music, which
is sometimes performed at concerts. The
opera was revived in Paris at the Théâtre du
Château d'Eau.

Henry VIII. (1882, *published* 1882), *opera
in* 4 *acts and* 5 *tableaux. Words by Léonce
Détroyat and Armand Silvestre. German
translation by Hermann Wolff. Italian trans-
lation by A. de Lauziéres. Piano score by
Léon Delahaye. Dedicated to M. Vancorbeil,
Director de l'Académie Nationale de Musique,
Paris, where the opera was produced on* 5*th*
March, 1883.

Act I contains six scenes. It opens with a
Prélude, of which the thematic material is
simply the Sixteenth Century subject, taken by
Saint-Saëns from the MSS. in the library at
Buckingham Palace. It reads :—

Considerable use is made of it throughout the opera.

The plot is concerned with the infatuation of the susceptible monarch for the beautiful lady-in-waiting of Katherine, Anne Boleyn, and is an embroidered edition—elaborately embroidered, one ought to say—of the historical facts.

The Spanish Ambassador, Don Gomez de Feria, and the Duke of Norfolk, have a conversation, in scene 1, in the course of which Don Gomez tells of an intrigue with Anne, and a letter which she has sent him. There is some rather graceful music for his love-sick description of her. This letter is the central subject of the final scene of the opera.

The librettists have not succeeded in making any of the characters very attractive.

Don Gomez is drawn as a sentimental fool; Anne Boleyn as a minx of the most designing type, and, as Katherine latterly describes her, "a girl without a heart." Katherine is pathetically sketched, but is frequently boring and depressing, so that one hardly marvels at the King's change of affections.

The King is represented as a domineering, somewhat irritating sensualist, a little given to self-pity, quite ignorant of fine feeling, and with a fondness for saying to anyone, who chances to be inconveniently present (including either of his wives), "Vous ici? Soit! Madame!"— an idea of brusque bonhomme that prepares

one, in a measure, for the last great scene
involving the King and the two Queens.

Katherine, very ill, and living in retirement
at Kimbolton after the marriage of Henry with
Anne, is visited by Anne, anxious to obtain the
compromising letter, which has come into the
possession of Katherine, by implorations, or,
failing these, by imprecations; but Anne fails
to recover it.

Henry arrives, at the end of this scene between the women, accompanied by Don Gomez.

Here, indeed, is a thrilling situation. The
King also wishes to get the letter. His methods
of gaining his desire take the shape of love-
making with Anne, before Katherine, who, in
her dire misery, calls to God for consolation and
strength to survive this culminating affront.

She does not, as the King expects, yield
up the letter in a fit of jealousy with the object
of harming her rival. Instead, she destroys it,
and worn out by the emotional stress of the
situation, dies without divulging her knowledge
of the import of the missive.

As in " Étienne Marcel," although hardly so
damnably, the strength of this ending is considerably weakened by the declaration of
Henry, that if he finds his suspicions of an
intrigue between Don Gomez and Anne were
correct, the hatchet will secure revenge !

Such a remark, although quite in keeping
with the vacillating braggadocio of the person-

ality that figures as Henry VIII., is particularly
nauseating in the circumstances; but what is of
real importance is that it quite spoils what
should have been an intensely dramatic dénouement. Quite conceivably it may have militated
against a revival of the opera in this country.
Otherwise, one can find no reason for the
neglect of this (musically) beautiful work.

The plot, if conventional, dealing, as it
does, with the eternal triangle, works onwards
interestingly to a conclusion. There is well-
written music, several beautiful melodies, and
ample spectacle, apart from that of the ballet-
divertissement which comes between Acts II.
and III.

This set of six dances in the ballet is sometimes performed as a suite, in the concert hall,
but at the production at Covent Garden the
ballet was omitted. Even then, the opera
would be long enough. It cannot be said that
the " Scottish " dances in the ballet (included,
probably, because of the fondness of Queen
Victoria for Balmoral) are happily conceived.
Her late Majesty was, as we know, a friend of
Saint-Saëns, but in these " Scottish " dances
exist an example of inspirational coercion that
should not have been attempted, even out of
respect for a friend. The Fourth No. of the
Suite, " Danse de la Gypsy," is, on the contrary,
in the composer's happiest vein, thus :—

Henry VIII. "Danse de la Gypsy"

Moderato quasi andantino

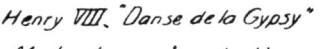

to an accompaniment of tympani and cymbals.
By the introduction of a second theme of barbaric character it achieves a striving, and colourful, climax; for in it is the sincere expression of
inherent idiom, plus experience, while the
"Scottish" dances are never anything but
counterfeit art.   The suite, as a whole, apparently constitutes an exception to the usual
Chameleon adaptability of the composer.   As
a matter of fact, part of the ballet was taken
from an unproduced one-act opéra-comique.

The structure of the music is on a symphonic
basis, thematic material undergoing development and certain melodic figures being associated with the appearance of certain members of
the *dramatis personæ*.

A graceful melodic figure—

Henry VIII. Don G. motif

Allegro non troppo

is especially associated with Don Gomez, for
example. To Henry, in Scene 4, Act I., is given
a fine solo—

Henry VIII. Solo: Henry
Sc. IV. Act I.

Larghetto

pp   Qui donc commande quand il aime

and he has a very passionate love-duet with
Anne; and the song in the final scene of the last
act already alluded to. Fanfares and grandiose
chords serve as reminders that he is very much
"le Roi."

The rôles of Katherine and Anne are of
almost equal importance. The music associated
with Katherine is often lachrymal, sometimes
pathetic, and on occasion, dramatic—as in the
last scene in which she dies, and in the last
scene (6) of the first act, where, with the others,
she watches the procession that accompanies
Buckingham to the scaffold, after she has, in
vain, pleaded with the King on his behalf.
Sotto-voce to her lamentations are heard the
love advances of the king to his new "woman"
—Anne—and the sound of the choir singing the
"De Profundis"! In scene 1 of the last act
one of the most beautiful, and originally harmonious, little airs in the whole opera is assigned
to Katherine, the alternating five-four and

three-four, and the abrupt key changes being
suggestively prophetic of her impending doom.

Anne has her greatest opportunity for display in the aria with which she occupies scene 3
of Act II., " Reine ! Je serai Reine ! "   The
melody is suave, *Andante con moto*, a little
florid. The harmony, very elaborate and
ornamented, reminds one of the old-fashioned
Italian florid arias for soprani.

The music in the letter scene between
Katherine and Anne is of a most animated
description.   The syncopated accompaniment
figure is charged with the seething restlessness
of scarcely bridled spite and jealousy.

In the big scene with the Papal Nuncio
expressive use is made of the Sixteenth Century theme, and there is much spectacular effect
in the scene in which the populace acclaim their
King although the Pope has excommunicated
him.

Even considering the blemishes alluded to
in this description of the opera, " Henry VIII."
is an art-creation that ought to be staged with
the regularity that its fine qualities merit. Since
the master himself sanctioned a performance,
during his lifetime, with the ballet omitted, that
manner of presentation might be adhered to,
and one of the weak features eliminated.

I commend the opera to the attention of those
active in the present operatic renaissance in
Great Britain.

The rôles arc arranged as follows :—Henry VIII., baritone; Don Gomez, tenor; Cardinal Compeggio, Papal legate, bass; Duke of Surrey, tenor; Duke of Norfolk, bass; Cranmer, Archbishop of Canterbury, bass; Katherine, soprano; Anne, mezzo-soprano.

Proserpine, drame-lyrique en quatre actes. Words, after the play by Auguste Vacquerie, by Louis Gallet. Produced at the Opéra-Comique, 15th March, 1887.

This adaptation by Gallet of the melodrama of Vacquerie contains excellent operatic possibilities of which Saint-Saëns made good use. It was most favourably received when produced, and one scene was encored.

The story is one of human passions, and portrays an incident of unrequited love in Italy of the Sixteenth Century.

Proserpine is a beautiful courtesan, who is madly in love with a young nobleman, Sabatino. Unfortunately for her, another woman, Angiola, has already enslaved the object of her desires, and is engaged to be married to him. She is, further, the sister of his friend, Renzo.

Prosperine enlists the sympathies of a bandit, Squarocca, and endeavours to do her worst to the lovers—at least to her rival.

There is an intense scene where she declares her love for Sabatino, and then tries to plunge her stiletto into Angiola. When prevented

M

from doing so by Sabatino, she plunges the weapon into her own bosom, and dies.

Originally, the dénouement permitted Proserpine to stab her rival, and then be killed by Sabatino, who snatched the weapon from her hand—a weak ending which the collaborators thought better of, fortunately, and when Saint Saëns went on a trip to Ceylon in 1891 he rewrote this part of the opera, the work in its final form being produced at the Opéra-Comique in 1899.

The music often becomes dramatically intense, and there is beautiful melody and gracious harmonies, particularly in an effective convent scene, which had to be repeated at the first production of the opera.

This scene was invented by Gallet to provide the peace, and quietness, necessary for contrast, from a musical point of view, amid so much passion and strife.   Vacquerie highly approved of this interpolation.

Ascanio, opera in five acts.   Words by Louis Gallet (founded on the drama, Benvenuto Cellini, by Paul Meurice).   Produced at the Académie Nationale de Musique, Paris, 5th March, 1890, and at the Opéra 21st March, 1890.

Ascanio is a pupil of Cellini.   He loves, and is loved, by Colombe, who is also loved by Cellini.   Here is again the triangle ; but by way

of variation, and complication, we have the
unrequited love of two other ladies—Scozzone,
who is devoted to Cellini, and the Duchesse
d'Etampes, who has conceived a passion for
Ascanio.

Here, indeed, is a veritable hell-broth as a
basis for plot-making, but the actual working
out strains credulity to breaking point, even for
a grand opera plot.

Benvenuto, learning of the love between his
pupil and Colombe, and of the lady's preference, retires from the field. Further, becoming
aware of danger threatening the much-loved
damsel from her two rivals, he decides to
smuggle her into a convent in an ornamental
chest which he has decorated for Ursuline nuns
there.

The Duchesse, however, arranges that the
reliquary shall rest at her house long enough to
suffocate the young rival who thus seeks to
escape her vengeance.

In the meantime, Scozzone, repenting of her
complicity in the horrible crime planned, and
full of the bitterness of a hopeless love, decides
to enter the box instead of Colombe.

There is a dramatic ending to all this plot
and counter-plot. Cellini, as a reward for his
art in decorating the reliquary, asks the King
(Francis I.) to consent to the marriage of the
two young lovers. The Duchesse, deeming that
the time has arrived to gloat over the fruit of

her revenge, opens the box and finds, to her
horror, that she has killed her fellow-accomplice
instead of their mutual rival.   In despair,
Cellini seeks retirement.

"Ascanio" suffered comparative eclipse
from 1891 until its revival, in Paris, in 1921—
a revival, which, as related in Part I., was
superintended by Saint-Saëns.

The music does not delve deeply into the
realms of the cruder emotions; but in the lighter
scenes it is gracious, and often brilliantly
orchestrated.   There is a ballet that contains
some of the composer's most attractive writing;
and spectacular effect is not lost sight of.

*Phryné, opéra-comique, in two acts.   Lib-
retto by L. Augé de Lassus.   Produced at the
Opéra-Comique, Paris, 24th May, 1893.*

This little work is concerned with the affairs
of a courtesan, Phryné, and her old and young
lovers, who happen to be uncle and nephew.
It is an amusing and gracefully conceived
opéra-comique, and bracketed, in performance,
with "La Princesse Jaune" or "Hélène' (see
Appendix), which last, although the inferior
work, would give greater contrast—would provide an evening performance.

*L'Ancêtre, lyrical drama in three acts.
Words by L. Augé de Lassus.   Produced at
Monte Carlo 24th February, 1906.*

The action is laid in Corsica.   It concerns a

vendetta in the relentless enactment of which
a fearful old woman, the Ancestress, devises
unwearied machinations. The plot is a re-hash
of the story of Romeo and Juliet, and therefore need not be detailed.

This opera achieved a great success at its
prémière. Its revival in Paris in 1911 was also
encouraging. The music is powerfully sketched
into the tragic picture, and in the lighter
moments it is charmingly fresh. I give this
brief resumé in the hope of stimulating the
interest of operatic managers and producers.

*Les Barbares, tragédie-lyrique, en trois actes
et prologue-symphonique. Words by Victorien
Sardou and P. B. Gheusi. Produced at the
Académie Nationale de Musique, 23rd Oct.,
1901.*

Saint-Saëns was enthusiastic about the
prospects and "story" of this work, but
although it was well received, it was not given
many times at the Opéra, upon its appearance
there.

The action centres upon the invasion of the
town of Orange by Teutonic barbarians.
Pillage is averted by Floria, a priestess of
Vesta, who secures the safety of the inhabitants
of the city by yielding to the advances of
Marcomir, the chief of the invaders. The
Roman consul, Euryalus, has been killed,
during warfare, by an unknown man, who, as

Livia, his widow, discovers, was Marcomir. A sense of poetic justice attends the murder of Marcomir, by Livia, who uses a piece of the weapon extracted from the body of Euryalus, with which to accomplish her revenge.

The structure of the music to this libretto is vigorous, and cyclic; and the innovation of a Symphonic Prologue, as an accompaniment to a verbal explanation of the action, is decidedly interesting.

That Saint-Saëns left only one ballet, " Javotte," is a matter for sincere regret, for the charm and grace of the music to the ballets in his operas denotes a special aptitude for this particular art-form. " Javotte " is in one act, and three tableaux, and was designed by J. L. Croze. It immediately gained favour upon its production at Lyons, on December 3rd, 1896, at the Grand Theatre; and it had very success-ful revivals at the Opéra-Comique, on 23rd October, 1899, and at the Opéra, on 5th February, 1909.

PART III

THEME VI

THE CHORAL WORKS

A choral work, the unpublished "Ode à Sainte Cécile" (1852), appeared at the beginning of the career of Saint-Saëns as a composer, and he returned intermittently to the writing of compositions for choir and orchestra of both sacred and secular character, until eight years before his death, when the oratorio, "The Promised Land" (1913), was produced at the Gloucester Musical Festival of that year.

In this final work of the oratorio class, and in some others of its kind, such as "Le Déluge," the feeling is often operatic, so that they provide a bridge, or connecting passage to the more spacious, and more plastic, environment of the stage, from the very restrained emotional opportunity of church music.

There is but one setting of the Mass, the *Messe Solennelle* (1856, pub. 1857), to the grandeur and beauty of which Liszt paid high tribute. He likened it to "a magnificent Gothic cathedral, in which Bach would conduct his orchestra," and regarded it as

comparable to the settings of Bach and Beethoven.

The *Oratorio de Noël* (1858) is another early work to which cathedral and oratory organists in this country might give regular attention. It was, of course, written at the time that Saint-Saëns received his appointment as organist at the Madeleine.

The music is melodious and simply devotional. There is beautiful part-writing, and opportunities for the soloists in a choir to distinguish themselves. The instrumental writing is for strings, harp, and organ.

The *Requiem Mass* (1878) is very elevated in its religious fervour, and contains a pathetically beautiful "Agnus Dei." The extraordinary fertility which enabled the composer to write it in eight days almost suggests an uncanny premonition of the tragic deaths of his infant children, which happened soon afterwards. The external circumstances merely point to coincidence.

"*Le Déluge*" (1875), *Poème Biblique en trois parties. Poème de L. Gallet. For solo voices, chorus, and orchestra.*

After a few bars of an expressive *Adagio*, a fugue, beginning—

Le Déluge (Prélude)

is introduced in the Prélude, which contains
some of the thematic material of the oratorio,
and is quiet and academic in style.   The
Prélude is, by the way, sometimes heard
as a separate composition.

The symphonic description of the flood is
a truly remarkable orchestral conception for
the time of its birth.

Beginning *ppp.*, and headed *Moderato-
quasi-andante-con-moto*, it works up to a
terrific sense of terrestrial, and celestial, dis-
turbance by means of chromatic and diatonic
(but chiefly the former) figures, arpeggi, and
scale passages.   These devices are in infinite
variety and are mostly written in demi-semiquavers and semiquavers.   A very full
orchestra is employed at this part of the work,
including five trombones and four low saxhorns.

In Part 1 Saint-Saëns contents himself with
string support for the voices (S., C., T., and B.
soli, and chorus) which are heard, largely in
recitative.

Part 3 produces an impression of the verdant
renewal of life in its pristine purity.

The musical allusion to the second flight of
the dove from the ark, and the return of
spring, is aptly (or banally, according to one's
view-point) signified by a distorted version of
the call of the cuckoo.

The oratorio concludes in hopeful and
joyous mood.

"The Promised Land," Oratorio, *Op.* 140. *Première à Gloucester Festival,* 1913. *Text arranged by Hermann Klein. Dedicated, by special permission, to Her Majesty Queen Alexandra by "her faithful and obedient servant, Camille Saint-Saëns."*

This splendid oratorio is in three parts. Mr. Hermann Klein, in his prefatory note, explains that "the text of the oratorio has been taken entirely from the books of Numbers and Deuteronomy, and from the Psalms."

Part 1 deals with the deliverance of the Israelites from Egypt, their sufferings in the desert, and the miracle of bringing the water from the rock.

Part 2 opens with the admonition of the Almighty to Moses and Aaron that "Because ye believed Me not, to sanctify Me in the eyes of the Children of Israel, therefore ye shall not bring this congregation into the land which I have given them."

Part 3 tells of the showing of the Promised Land, by the Lord, to Moses from the hills; and of the death of the patriarch. "So Moses, the servant of the Lord, died there according to the word of the Lord. And He buried him in a valley in the land of Moab; but no man knoweth his sepulchre unto this day."

Discarding the picturesque Jewish narratives that explain why Moses was not allowed to enter Canaan, Mr. Hermann Klein has

based his text on the view that Moses' special
sin lay in the *smiting* of the rock with his rod,
instead of speaking to it, as commanded by
God (Numbers xx, 8).

" The Promised Land " is composed for soli
(S., C., T., and B.), chorus, and orchestra.
When writing it the composer evidently
had the models of Handel, Bach, and
Beethoven, in the same form, in mind.

The result is an eminently musicianly, and
often impressive emotional, conception of the
text.   There is nothing, one imagines, to shock
the most enthusiastic " Messiah" and " Elijah"
Choral Societies upon a first acquaintance with
the score; and why, in the cause of variety and
good music, we do not hear " The Promised
Land" often, is obscure.   Conductors of
Choral Societies will probably remark that
"people don't know it !" Tut, tut ! *mes amis* ! !
There was a time, I suppose, when even " The
Messiah " was "not known "; and also, when
you yourselves did not know a note from a rest
or a bar line !

Althought the master has largely followed
classical precedent in his style of writing,
there is ample evidence of his individuality; of
the Saint-Saëns of " Samson et Dalila " even.

The sixth number of Part 1, for vocal trio
and choir, is thoroughly characteristic; and
still more so is the vocal quintet (No. 9 of
Part 2), which has an accompaniment figure

tremendously significant of the Divine Anger alluded to in the words. The orchestral scoring for the allusion to the bursting forth, and flowing, of the water from the rock is reminiscent of the water music in " Le Déluge."

The No. 12 of Part 3, "The Song of Moses," a fine, broad melody, simply harmonised, is what the brief song reviewers would term "well laid out" for voice (bass), but it is artistically disappointing, bearing in mind its composer. In No. 13 is a fair example of Saint-Saëns as a colourist. The impression of awe and mystery suggested by the command of the Almighty, to the patriarch, to "Get thee up into Mount Abarim, and behold the Land," etc., is realized in a wonderful manner by the composer.

PART III

THEME VII

LITERARY WORKS

The composer who appears in the rôle of author, on occasion, is a figure by no means without precedent in the history of musical art. Among those who have also become famous in the sister art, the names of Schumann, Berlioz, and Wagner occur instantly to the memory. The literary work of Saint-Saëns, however, has not been primarily concerned with any special sphere of writing. In literature, as in music, he has expressed himself in most diverse forms. He wrote philosophy and metaphysics, drama and comedy, poetry and religion and science, and, of course, music criticism, with the same degree of spontaneity that he composed concertos, instrumental and vocal solos, symphonies, operas and opéra-comique, cantatas, oratorios, and music-drama.

A volume might easily be devoted to the critical study of his numerous letters, his poems, and his general literary output, for his

remarks are entertaining, his expression provocative of thought, and illuminated by penetratingly clear conclusions, and suggestions, that must sometimes have been more the outcome of intuition than of actual, detailed knowledge. A naïve style of engaging freshness characterises his literary work, much as the instinctive feeling for colour gives to his musical compositions an individualism that is unmistakable.

Consider this extract,* for instance, from the " École Buissonière," *a propos* Berlioz's " Requiem " :—

" The reading of the score of Berlioz's ' Requiem ' makes it appear singularly old-fashioned, but this is true of most of the romantic dramas, which, like the ' Requiem,' show up better in actual performance. It is easy to rail at the vehemence of the Romanticists, but it is not so easy to equal the effect of ' Hernani,' ' Lucrece Borgia,' and the Symphonie fantastique on the public. For with all their faults these works had a marvellous success. The truth is that their vehemence was sincere and not artificial. The Romanticists had faith in their works, and there is nothing like faith to produce lasting results.''

Further on, in the same essay, is an example of the impatience with the usual attitude of the world towards the creative artist that is of child-like petulance :—

" He was astonished at the lack of sympathy, and even actual hostility, that he encountered (i.e., in the perform-

* From the English translation, " Musical Memories."

ance of the ' Requiem '). It would have been more astonishing if he had experienced anything else."

Clearly, when writing this, Saint-Saëns had a vivid remembrance of the tribulations that beset the production of his opera " L'Timbre d'Argent."

The following passage, from the conclusion of the same essay as the above extracts, is of disarming candour :—

" Berlioz was a genius, not a scholar. The word genius tells the whole story. Berlioz wrote badly (for voices). He maltreated voices and sometimes permitted himself the strangest freaks. Nevertheless, he is one of the commanding figures of musical art. His great works remind us of the Alps with their forests, glaciers, sunlight, waterfalls and chasms. There are people who do not like the Alps. So much the worse for them."

In the essay devoted to his friend Seghers is a passage uncommonly like the expression of the views of a very modern student of music of to-day upon what exactly constitutes music :

" Someone has said lately that where there is no feeling there is no music. We could, however, cite many passages of music which are absolutely lacking in emotion, and which are beautiful nevertheless from the point of view of pure æsthetic beauty.

" But what am I saying? Painting goes its own way and emotion, feeling, and passion are evoked by the least landscape. Maurice Barrès brought in this fashion and he could even see passion in rocks. Happy is he who can follow him there."

Although he dealt with the subject of his choice, logically, for the time being, his general

art-outlook was often contradictory. Probably this was traceable to the ceaseless activity of his brain during waking hours, whether at work or during his brief, but frequent, spells of recreation; and to his impatience against restraint of any kind, more especially against restraint of the intellect. Heaven may be reached by more than one route, and so also may the Valhalla towards which all serious artists strive more or less consciously.

In the first collection of his articles issued by C. Lévy, in 1885, under the title " Harmonie et Mélodie," we find such an idea expressed :—

(*Apropos* Wagner). " Not only do I not deny him, but I glory in having studied him and profited by him, as it was my right and my duty. I have done the same as regards Sebastian Bach, Haydn, Beethoven, Mozart, and all the masters of all the schools. I do not, on that account, consider myself obliged to say, of each one of them, that he alone is god, and that I am his prophet. In reality, it is neither Bach, nor Beethoven, nor Wagner whom I love; it is art. I am an eclectic. This is perhaps a great defect, but it is impossible for me to correct it; one cannot alter one's nature. Again, I love liberty passionately, and cannot bear to have admirations imposed upon me. Enthusiasms to order freeze the blood in my veins, and render me incapable of appreciating the most beautiful works."

Comparing the above quotation with the following one, from " Anarchy in Music " (École Buissonière), one realises that Saint-Saëns did not always appreciate the other fellow's point of view; or, rather, that although

his intelligence saw it, his natural sympathies,
lying in the opposite direction, he was inclined
to deny that it might also contain truth :—

" The man with a ' developed taste ' is not the one who
knows how to get new and unexpected results by passing
from one key to another, as the great Richard did in ' Die
Meistersinger,' but rather the man who abandons all keys,
and piles up dissonances which he neither introduces nor
concludes, and who, as a result grunts his way through
music as a pig through a flower garden.

" Possibly they may go further still.   There seems no
reason why they should linger on the way to untrammelled
freedom, or restrict themselves within a scale.   The
boundless empire of sound is at their disposal, and let
them profit by it.   That is what dogs do when they bay at
the moon, cats when they mew, and birds when they sing.
A German has written a book to prove that the birds sing
false.   Of course he is wrong, for they do not sing false.
If they did, their songs would not sound agreeable to us.
They sing outside of scales, and it is delightful, but that is
not man-made art."

Discussing the evolution of opera, from those
of the Rossini genre, with their overtures
and *crescendo*, which, in spirit, preserve the
custom of the showman banging his drum
noisily, and shouting vociferously outside his
booth, ere the show (which has been "just
a-goin' to begin " for perhaps an hour), actually
does begin, to the music-drama of Wagner,
where the overture is curtailed to, or rather,
replaced by, a prélude ; and then to the omission,
even of the prélude, by Verdi and Strauss,
he concludes, alluding to the suppression of
the prélude, " It is like a dinner without soup."

N

Yet this model is one that he has adhered to himself in " Samson et Dalila."

One might quote many examples to illustrate his often amusing manner of expression, but a few must suffice.

Writing of Delsarte ("École Buissonière "), he observes :—

" . . . for even if masterpieces are presented badly, there is always something left. Besides, both the singer (Delsarte) and his hearer had Faith. He had a way of pronouncing ' Gluck ' which aroused expectation even before one heard a note."

Again, in the same volume, he writes, regarding the special métiers of Liszt and of Gounod :

" As there is an *odor di femina,* there is a *parfum d'eglise,* well known to Catholics. Gounod's oratorios are impregnated with this, while it is found in ' Chistus ' (of Liszt) very, very feebly, if at all."

He was fond of directing his caustic wit against sham and affectations of all kinds. Delsarte, in the article from which the quotation above is given, receives a fair meed of this form of attention.

In " Portraits et Souvenirs " (1899), another collection of articles, many of which give intimate pen-studies of the famous composers and executants whom the master knew in the course of his long life, one finds this, regarding the futuristic craze, as manifested in music :—

" The situation is reversed. Amateurs who refused to make the least effort to understand music have become possessed by a passion for the obscure and the incom-

prehensible. They are irritated or disdainful if the instruments of the orchestra do not run from one side to the other like poisoned rats; at a simple accompaniment they shrug their shoulders.''

Further (in " École Buissonière) he writes :

" An artistic people is recognized by their ignorance of ' objects of art,' for in such an environment art is everywhere. An artistic people no more dreams of creating art than a great nobleman of consciously exhibiting a distinguished manner. Distinction lies in his slightest mannerism without his being conscious of the fact. So, among artistic peoples, the most humble and ordinary objects have style."

Regarding the "show" conductor he is, one feels, a little lacking in sympathetic insight. Quite conceivably a very sincere musician, and a very sincere artist, may be permitted to put something of his own individuality into a work which he is conducting—if it is allowable for an executive solo artist to do so, as Saint-Saëns implies on many occasions, but especially in his exceedingly sympathetic reminiscences of Pauline Viardot.

On the other hand, one gladly joins issue in the following attack upon the disgusting abuse of his position which the "show" conductor is prone to make as a result of his own, and his audiences' love of sensation :—

" But the orchestra conductors have to be taken into account. In our day, these gentlemen are *virtuosi*. Their personalities are not subservient to the music, but the music to them. It is the spring-board on which they perform and parade their all-embracing personalities. They

add their own inventions to the author's meaning. Sometimes they draw out the wind instruments so that the musicians have to cut a phrase at the end to catch their breath ; again, they affect a mad and unrestrained rapidity which allows time neither to play nor to hear the sounds. They hurry, or retard the pace, for no reason besides their individual caprice.''

But I must cease from quotations in this vein or the casual reader may conclude that Saint-Saëns was an uncharitable and bitter old man, than which there could hardly be a greater misapprehension. In Parts I. and II. of this book I have endeavoured to give an impression of his personality : here we are concerned with the formation of an idea of his literary manner.

His use of poetical imagery is effective, but not excessive. It is invariably refined, and does not descend to fulsomeness. Nor is the metaphor that is mixed found in his pages.

Comparing the genius and artistic outlook of Berlioz and Wagner, he writes ("École Buissonière ") :—

" . . . if there is a surprising page in the history of music, it is the persistent affectation of classing Berlioz and Wagner together . . . Berlioz opened to the orchestra the doors to a new world. Wagner hurled himself into this unknown country, and found numerous lands to till there.''

" The rose with its fresh colour and its perfume is, in its way, as precious as the sturdy oak. Art has a place for artists of all kinds, and no one should flatter himself that he is the only one who is capable of covering the entire field of art.''

Then, *a propos*, the assumed poor musical taste of the general public :—

"One day I was walking in a garden. There was a bandstand, and musicians were playing some sort of music. The crowd was indifferent, and passed by without paying the slightest attention. Suddenly there sounded the first notes of the delightful *Andante* of Beethoven's Symphony in D—a flower of spring with a delicate perfume. At the first notes all walking and talking ceased."

The following quotations ("Harmonie et Mélodie") demonstrate his happy gift of allusion :—

"... from the heights of the last act of Gotterdammerung, the entire work appears in its almost supernatural immensity, like the chain of the Alps seen from the summit of Mont Blanc."

"... a kind of musical Alfred de Musset, Schumann is the man of exquisite things; he knows how to be great in small styles and in small frameworks."

But for the art of Schumann in general, and for his works as a music critic, Saint-Saëns had scant regard.

Another volume, similar in composition to those already considered, is entitled "Au Courant de la Vie." It discusses many subjects, from animals, chiefly domestic, of which the composer was very fond, to incidents and reminiscences of travel which, by the way, are also referred to in the "École Buissonière."

"Problèmes et Mystères" (1894) gives the student of the master's life, and, incidentally, of psychology, an insight into the outlook of a cultured and highly intellectual brain towards the conclusion of a long and active life. A very different thing indeed from the "recollections"

of vain things and years of frivolling, be-sprinkled with erotic pen-portraits of the Great, encountered in their aimless gyrations through Life, with which the human butterflies of the world are wont, in these days, to make a frantic endeavour to do something creative before the end; something which may bear their names to posterity.

Compare the lofty idealism, and beautiful conclusions, upon the meaning of life, arrived at by Saint-Saëns, with the cul-de-sac notions of the type of senile abortion referred to :—

" The joys offered us by Nature, which she does not refuse, even to those least favoured among us; that which is procured by the discovery of new truths; the aesthetic enjoyment of Art; the spectacle of sufferings relieved, and the effort to suppress them as much as possible—all this may suffice for the happiness of life."

APPENDIX

APPENDIX

The compositions of Saint-Saëns are mostly published by A. Durand et fils, 4, Place de la Madeleine, Paris. Exceptions to this rule, in the list appended, have the publishers' name in parenthesis. Some of the works are unnumbered.

THE CONCERTOS.

Title.	No.	Composed and Published.	Début.	Incidents.
Concerto in D, pianoforte	Op. 17	1858-9, pub. 1875	Paris	Dedicated to Mme. Alfred Jaël.
Ditto, in G minor	Op. 22	1868, pub. 1868		Dedicated to Mme. A. de Villers, née de Haber. Composer soloist at début; Rubinstein conductor.
3rd ditto, in E flat	Op. 29	1869, pub. 1875		Dedicated to M. E. M. Delaborde.
4th ditto, in C minor	Op. 44	1875, pub. 1877		Dedicated to M. Antoine Door.
5th ditto, in F	Op. 103	1896, pub. 1896		Dedicated to M. Louis Diémer. Composed during a visit to Egypt.
1st Concerto in A, for violin and orch.	Op. 20	1859, pub. 1868 (Hamelle)		Dedicated to Sarasate.
2nd ditto, in C	Op. 58	1858, pub. 1879		Dedicated to Sarasate.
3rd ditto, in B minor	Op. 61	1880, pub. 1881		Dedicated to Sarasate.
1st Concerto, in A minor, 'cello and orchestra	Op. 33	1872, pub. 1873		Dedicated to M. Auguste Tolbeque, who played it often.
2nd ditto, in D minor	Op. 119	1902, pub. 1902		Dedicated to M. Joseph Hollman.

THE SYMPHONIES AND SYMPHONIC POEMS.

Title.	No.	Composed and Published.	Début.	Incidents.
1st Symphony, in E flat ...	Op. 2 ...	1853, pub. 1855 ...	Paris ...	Dedicated to M. F. Seghers. Gounod and Berlioz discussed the work in the presence of Saint-Saëns unaware it was his. Produced anonymously.
2nd ditto, in F ...	...	1856, not published		
3rd ditto, in D ...	...	1859, not published		
4th ditto, in A minor ...	Op. 55 ...	1859, pub. 1878 ...	Paris	Dedicated to M. J. Pasdeloup. Referred to, and published as, the " Second " Symphony.
5th ditto, in C minor ...	Op. 78 ...	1886, pub. 1886 ...	London ...	Dedicated to Liszt. Produced by Royal Philharmonic Society. Début conducted by composer. Referred to, and published as, the " Third " Symphony.
Le Rouet d'Omphale, Poème symphonique ...	Op. 31 ...	1871, pub. 1872 ...	...	Dedicated to Mdlle. Augusta Holmès.
Phaéton, Poème symphonique ...	Op. 39 ...	1873, pub. 1875 ...	...	Dedicated to Mme. Berthe Pochet, née de Tinan.
Danse Macabre ditto ...	Op. 40 ...	1874, pub. 1875 ...		
La Jeunesse d'Hercule ditto ...	Op. 50 ...	1877, pub. 1877 ...	...	Dedicated to M. Henri Duparc.

CHAMBER MUSIC.

Title.	No.	Composed and Published.	Début.	Incidents.
Quintet, pianoforte and strings...	Op. 14	1855, pub. 1865 (Hamelle)	...	Dedicated to M. Alfred Lamarche. Conceived during a holiday in the Pyrenees.
Trio, in F, pianoforte, violin, 'cello	Op. 18	1863, pub. 1867 (Hamelle)	...	
2nd Trio, in E minor, ditto	Op. 92	1892, pub. 1892	...	
Quartet for strings, No. 1 (2 violins, viola, 'cello)	Op. 112	1899, pub. 1899	...	Dedicated to Ysaÿe.
Ditto, No 2, ditto ditto	Op. 153	1919, pub. 1919	Paris	
Quartet, in B flat, for pianoforte, violin, viola, 'cello	Op. 41	1875, pub. 1875	...	Dedicated to M. Jacques Durand.
Sonata, No. 1, in C minor pianoforte and 'cello	Op. 32	1872, pub. 1873	...	Performed at the 25th (London) anniversary concert, given 7.6.1910, by Hollman, in Queen's Hall, the composer at the pianoforte.
Ditto, No. 2, in F ditto	Op. 123	1905, pub. 1905	...	
Sonata, No. 1, violin and pianoforte	Op. 75	1885, pub. 1885	...	Dedicated to M. Jules Griset.
Ditto, No. 2, in E flat ditto	Op. 102	1896, pub. 1896	...	
Septet, for trumpet, two violins, viola, 'cello, double bass, and pianoforte	Op. 65	1881, pub. 1881	Paris	
Prière, 'cello and organ	Op. 158	1920	...	
Sérénade, pianoforte, organ, violin, viola (or 'cello)	Op. 15	1866, pub. 1868 (Choudens)	...	
Suite, for 'cello and pianoforte	Op. 16	1862, pub. 1866 (Hamelle)	...	Written for a Society known as "La Trompette." Included in programme of celebration concert above mentioned.

CHAMBER MUSIC—(*Continued*).

161

Title.	No.	Composed and Published.	Début.	Incidents.
Romance, pianoforte, organ, violin and violin	Op. 27	... 1868, pub. 1868	...	
Berceuse, in B flat, for pianoforte	Op. 38	... 1871, pub. 1874	...	
Allegro appassionato, for 'cello and pianoforte	Op. 43	... 1875, pub. 1875	...	
Romance, in C, for violin and pianoforte	Op. 48	... 1874, pub. 1876	...	
Romance, in D, 'cello and pianoforte	Op. 51	... 1877, pub. 1877	...	
"Wedding-cake" valse-caprice, pianoforte and strings	Op. 76	... 1885, pub. 1886	...	
Caprice sur des airs Danois et Russes, for pianoforte, flute, oboe, and clarinet	Op. 79	... 1887, pub. 1887	...	
Le Cygne. Mélodie, for 'cello or violin and pianoforte and solo	From. Op. unpublished	pub. 1887	...	... The only published number from the orchestral work, " Le Carnaval des animaux."
Chant Saphique, 'cello and pianoforte	Op. 91	... 1892, pub. 1892	...	
Moreau de Concert, horn and pianoforte	Op. 94	... 1887, pub. 1893	...	
Barcarolle, violin, 'cello, harmonium, and pianoforte	Op. 108	... 1898, pub. 1898	...	
Fantaisie, violin and harp	Op. 124	... 1907, pub. 1907	...	
Elégie, violin and pianoforte	Op. 143	... 1915, pub. 1915	...	
Cavatine, tenor trombone and piano	Op. 144	...		

WORKS, OTHER THAN CONCERTOS, FOR SOLO INSTRUMENTS & ORCHESTRA.

Title.	No.	Composed and Published.	Début.	Incidents.
Fantaisie, "Africa," pianoforte and orchestra	Op. 89	1891, pub. 1891 ...		
Allegro appassionato, pianoforte and orchestra	Op. 70	1884, pub. 1884 ...		
Rapsodie d'Auvergne, pianoforte and orchestra	Op. 73	1884, pub. 1884 ...		
Introduction et Rondo capriccioso for violin and orchestra	Op. 28	1863, pub. 1870 ...		
Morceau de Concert, violin and orchestra	Op. 62	1880, pub. 1881 ...		
Havanaise, violin and orchestra	Op. 83	1887, pub. 1888 ...		
Caprice Andalous, violin & orch.	Op. 122	1904, pub. 1904 ...		
La Muse et la Poëte, violin, 'cello, and orchestra (or pianoforte)	Op. 132	1909, pub. 1910 ...	London ...	Specially composed for the Celebration Concert at Queen's Hall, 7.6.1910, and played then by Ysaÿe and Hollman.
Tarantelle, flute and clarinet and orchestra	Op. 6	1857, pub. 1857 ...	Paris. ...	This is the composition that was introduced (anonymously) by Rossini at his house. (See Part I.)
Romance, in F, horn and orch.	Op. 36	1874, pub. 1874 ...		
Romance, in D flat, flute & orch.	Op. 37	1871, pub. 1874 ...		
Morceau de Concert, harp and orchestra	Op. 154	1919, pub. 1919 ...		
Cyprès et Lauriers, organ and orchestra	Op. 156	1919 ...		

VARIOUS ORCHESTRAL WORKS.

Title.	No.	Composed and Published.	Début.	Incidents.
Overture, " Spartacus "		1863, unpublished		
Suite. (1) Prélude. (2) Sarabande. (3) Gavotte. (4) Romance. (5) Finale.	Op. 49	1863, pub. 1877 ...		
Marche Héroïque	Op. 34	1871, pub. 1871 ...	Paris	Dedicated to the memory of Henri Regnault, a friend, killed during the Seige of Paris.
Suite Algérienne. (1) Prélude. (2) Rapsodie Mauresque. (3) Rêverie du Soir. (4) Marche Militaire-français.	Op. 60	1880, pub. 1881 ...		
Une nuit à Lisbonne, Barcarolle for orchestra	Op. 63	1880, pub. 1881 ...		
La Jota Aragonese	Op. 64	1880, pub. 1881 ...		
Hymn à Victor Hugo, for orchestra, including 8 harps, 8 trumpets, and chorus ad lib.	Op. 69	1881, pub. 1884 ...	Paris	Performed at the Trocadéro at a celebration in honour of Hugo. The incident led to the re-union of the two friends (Saint-Saëns and Hugo), who had been estranged for years. (See Part I).
Le Carnaval des Animaux				Unpublished, except for the melody, " Le Cygne."
Sarabande et Rigaudon	Op. 93	1892, pub. 1892 ...		

VARIOUS ORCHESTRAL WORKS—(Continued).

Title.	No.	Composed and Published.	Début.	Incidents.
Coronation March	... Op. 117	... 1902, pub. 1902	... London	... Written for the Coronation of the late King Edward VII, containing the Sixteenth Century theme used in the opera, "Henry VIII."
Ouverture de Fête	... Op. 133	... 1909, pub. 1910	...	
Marche Interalliée	... Op. 155	... 1919, pub. 1919	...	... To celebrate the end of the war.

WORKS FOR MILITARY BAND.

Orient et Occident	... Op. 25	... 1869, pub. 1870	...	
Hymne Franco-Espagnol	...	... 1900, pub. 1901	...	
Sur les bords du nil (Marche Militaire)	... Op. 125	... 1908, pub. 1908	...	

COMPOSITIONS FOR PIANO (Solo & Duo).

Six Bagatelles	solo Op. 3	... 1855, pub. 1856	...	
First Mazurka	... Op. 21	... 1868, pub. 1868	...	
Second ,,	... Op. 24	... 1871, pub. 1872	...	
Third ,,	... Op. 66	... 1882, pub. 1883	...	
Gavotte	... Op. 23	... 1871, pub. 1872	...	
Romance sans Paroles	... Op. ?	... 1871, pub. 1872	... (Joubert)	
Six Etudes (1st book)	... Op. 52	... 1877, pub. 1877	...	
,, ,, (2nd book)	... Op. 111	... 1899, pub. 1899	...	
Menuet et Valse	... Op. 56	... 1878, pub. 1878	...	
Album	... Op. 72	... 1884, pub. 1884	...	

(1) Prélude (2) Carillon
(3) Toccata (4) Valse
(5) Chanson Napolitaine
(6) Finale

COMPOSITIONS FOR PIANO (Solo & Duo)—(*Continued*).

Title.	No.	Composed and Published.	Début.	Incidents.
Souvenir d'Italie	solo	Op. 80 ... 1887, pub. 1887 ...		
Les Cloches du Soir	,,	Op. 85 ... 1889, pub. 1889 ...		
Valse Canariote	,,	Op. 88 ... 1890, pub. 1890 ...		
Valse Mignon	,,	Op. 104 ... 1896, pub. 1896 ...		
Valse Nonchalante	,,	Op. 110 ... 1898, pub. 1898 ...		
Valse Langoureuse	,,	Op. 120 ... 1903, pub. 1903 ...		
Suite	,,	Op. 90 ... 1891, pub. 1891 ...		
(1) Prélude et Fugue				
(2) Menuet (3) Gavotte				
(4) Gigue				
Thème Varié	,,	Op. 97 ... 1894, pub. 1894 ...		
Souvenir d'Ismalaïa	,,	Op. 100 ... 1895, pub. 1895 ...		
Duettino 1 pianoforte, 4 hands		Op. 11 ... 1855, pub. 1861 ... (Hamelle)		
Koënig Harald Harfagar	,,	Op. 59 ... 1880, pub. 1880 ... (Bote & Boch, Berlin)		... After the ballad by Heine.
Feuillet d'Album	,,	Op. 81 ... 1887, pub. 1887 ...		
Pas redoublé	,,	Op. 86 ... 1887, pub. 1890 ...		
Berceuse	,,	Op. 105 ... 1896, pub. 1896 ...		
Variations sur un thème	,,	Op. 35 ... 1874, pub. 1874 ...		
de Beethoven				
2 pianofortes, 4 hands				
Polonaise	,,	Op. 77 ... 1886, pub. 1886 ...		
Scherzo	,,	Op. 87 ... 1889, pub. 1890 ...		
Caprice Arabe	,,	Op. 96 ... 1894, pub. 1894 ...		
Caprice Héroïque	,,	Op. 106 ... 1898, pub. 1898 ...		... Performed at the Celebration Concert in London, 7.6.1910, by the composer and the late M. Pugno.
Vers la Victoire	...	Op. 152 ... 1919, pub. 1919 ...		

COMPOSITION FOR HARP (SOLO).

Title.	No.	Composed and Published.	Début	Incidents.
Fantaisie	... Op. 95	... 1893; pub. 1893	...	

COMPOSITIONS FOR ORGAN.

Title.	No.	Composed and Published.	Début	Incidents.
Fantaisie No. 1	... Op. ?	... 1856, pub. 1875 (Costallat)	...	
„ No. 2	... Op. 101	... 1895, pub. 1895	...	
„ No. 3	... Op. 137	...	...	
„ No. 4	... Op. 157	...	...	
Trois Rapsodies sur des cantiques Bretons	Op. 7	... 1866, pub 1866	...	... Two of these rapsodies are published for orchestra in an amplified version under the same Op. No.
Marche Religieuse	... Op. 107	... 1897, pub. 1898	...	
Trois Préludes et Fugues (1st book)	... Op. 99	... 1894, pub. 1894	...	
„ „ (2nd book)	Op. 109	... 1898, pub. 1898	...	
Bénédiction Nuptiale	... Op. 9	... 1859, pub. 1866	...	... Performed in Westminster Abbey in February, 1922, at the Wedding of H.R.H. Princess Mary and Viscount Lascelles.
Sept Improvisations pour Grand Orgue Op. 150				

COMPOSITIONS FOR HARMONIUM.

Title.	No.	Composed and Published.	Début	Incidents.
Trois Morceaux (1) Meditation (2) Barcarolle (3) Prière	Op. 1	... 1852, pub. 1858 (Girod)	...	
Six duos for harmonium and pianoforte	Op. 8	... 1858, pub. 1858 (Fromont)	...	
Elévation ou Communion	... Op. 13	... 1865, pub. 1865	...	

WORKS COMPOSED FOR THE STAGE.

Title.	No.	Composed and Published.	Début.	Incidents.
La Princesse Jaune, Opéra- comique, 1 act	Op. 30	1872, pub. 1872	Paris	Première l'Opéra - Comique, 12.6.1872.
Le Timbre d'Argent, Drame- lyrique, 4 acts	Op. ?	1875-7, pub. by (Choudens)	Paris	Première Théâtre - Lyrique, 23.2.1877.
Samson et Dalila, Opéra, 3 acts	Op. 47	1868-77, pub. 1877	Weimar	Première Grand Ducal Théâtre, Weimar, 2.12.77.
Étienne Marcel, Opéra, 4 acts	Op. ?	1877-8, pub. 1878	Lyons	Première Grand Théâtre, Lyons, 8.2.1879.
Henry VIII., Opéra, 4 acts	Op. ?	1882, pub. 1882	Paris	Première Académie Nationale de Musique, Paris, 5.3.1883.
Proserpine, Drame-lyrique, 4 acts	Op. ?	1886-7, pub. 1887	Paris	Première l'Opéra - Comique, Paris, 16.3.1887.
Ascanio, Opéra, 5 acts	Op. ?	1888, pub. 1890	Paris	Première l'Opéra, 21.3.1890. Revived there also in 1921.
Phryné, Opéra-comique, 2 acts	Op. ?	1892-3, pub. 1893	Paris	Première l'Opéra - Comique, 24.5.1893.
Frédégonde, Drame - lyrique, 5 acts	Op. ?	1895, pub. 1895 Société d'Edition.	Paris	Première l'Opéra, 18.12.1895. The opera was merely completed by Saint-Saëns, being the creation of a friend, Ernest Guiraud.
Les Barbares, Tragédie-lyrique, 3 acts and a prologue	Op. ?	1901, pub. 1901	Paris	Première l'Opéra, 23.10.1901.
Hélène, Poème-lyrique, 1 act	Op. ?	1903, pub. 1904	Monte Carlo.	Première Théâtre de Monte Carlo, 18.1.1904.
L'Ancêtre, Drame-lyrique, 3 acts	Op. ?	1905, pub. 1906	Monte Carlo.	Première Théâtre de Monte Carlo, 24.2.1906.

WORKS COMPOSED FOR THE STAGE—(Continued).

Title.	No.	Composed and Published.	Début.	Incidents.
Déjanire	Op. ?	1910, pub. 1911	Monte Carlo.	Première Théâtre de Monte Carlo, 14.3.1911. An adaptation by Saint-Saëns of the libretto and music for Gallet's tragedy, "Déjanire," produced at Béziers in 1898.
Gabriella di Vergy, Opéra-burlesque		1885, not published	Paris	Produced privately and at "La Trompette" (see Part I.)
La blouse et L'Habit or Le fils de la Revolution		Not published		Produced privately (see Part II.)
Javotte, Ballet, 1 act and 3 tableaux (J. L. Croze)	3 Op.	1896, pub. 1896	Lyons	Première Grand Théâtre, Lyons, 3.12.1896.

INCIDENTAL MUSIC TO THE FOLLOWING PRODUCTIONS.

Title.	No.	Composed and Published.	Début.	Incidents.
Déjanire, Tragédie-lyrique, 4 acts (Louis Gallet)		1898, pub. 1898	Béziers	Première Théâtre des Arènes, Béziers, 28.8.1898.
Parysatis, Drame-lyrique, 3 acts (Mme. Jane Dieulafoy)		1902, pub. 1902	Béziers	Première Théâtre des Arènes, Béziers, 17.8.1902.
Antigone, Tragédie, 5 acts (Paul Meurice and A. Vacquerie, after Sopocles)		1893, pub. 1893	Paris	Première Théâtre Français, 21.11.1894.
Andromaque, Tragédie, 5 acts (Jean Racine)		1902, pub. 1902	Paris	Première Théâtre Sarah Bernhardt, 7.2.1903.
L'assassinat du duc de Guise, Tableau d'histoire (Henri Lavedau)		1908, pub. 1908	Paris	Première Salle Charras, 1908.

661

INCIDENTAL MUSIC TO THE FOLLOWING PRODUCTIONS—(*Continued*).

Title.	No.	Composed and Published.	Début.	Incidents.
La fille du tourneur d'ivoire, Poème-antique, 2 acts (Mme. Henry Ferrare, after the novel by Madame Jean Bertheroy)	...	1909	... Paris	... At a special private matinée, 12.6.1909.
La Foi, Trois Tableau Symphonique (after Brieux's drama)	...	Op. 130 ... 1910, pub. 1910 ...		

CHORAL WORKS.

Title.	No.	Composed and Published.	Incidents.
Ode à Sainte Cécile	Op. ?	1852, unpublished...	
Scène d'Horace (P. Corneille), soprano, baritone, & orchestra	Op. 10	1860, pub. 1861 ...	
Les Noces de Prométhée (Romain Cornut), solo, choir, and orch.	Op. 19	1867, pub. 1867 ... (Hamelle)	
Cantate, for centenary birth of Hoche (words Em. Deschamps)		1868, unpublished...	... Privately produced, 24.6.1868.
Le Déluge, Poème Biblique, in 3 parts, soli, chorus, and orchestra (words Louis Gallet)	Op. 45	1875, pub. 1876 ...	
La Lyre et La Harpe (Victor Hugo), ode for soli, chorus, and orchestra (English version of Hugo's poem by Sydney Samuel and James Donzel)	Op. 57	1879, pub. 1879 ...	Birmingham. Produced at the Birmingham Musical Festival, 1879.
Nuit Persane (Armand Renaud)	Op. 26 (bis.)	1891, pub. 1892 ...	
La Fiancée du Timbalier (Hugo), Ballade for mezzo-soprano and orchestra	Op. 82	1887, pub. 1888 ...	
Pallas Athéné (J. L. Croze), soprano and orchestra	Op. ?	1894, pub. 1894 ...	

CHORAL WORKS—(Continued).

Title.	No.	Composed and Published.	Début.	Incidents.
Lever de soleil sur le nil (C. Saint-Saëns), contralto and orchestra	Op. ?	1898, pub. 1898	...	...
La Nuit (G. Audigier), soprano solo, female chorus, and orch.	Op. 114	1900, pub. 1900	...	...
Le Feu Céleste (Armand Sil-vestre), Cantata for soprano, chorus, orchestra, organ, and a reciter	Op. 115	1900, pub. 1900	Paris	In praise of electricity. Produced at the opening concert, Paris Exhibition, May, 1900.
Lola (Stephan Bordèse), Scène dramatique for two personages and orchestra	Op. 116	1900, pub. 1900	...	...
La Gloire de Corneille (Seb. C. Lecomte), Cantata, soli, chorus, and orchestra	Op. 126	1906, pub. 1906	...	...
The Promised Land (Hermann Klein), Oratorio, soli, chorus, and orchestra	Op. 140	1913, pub. 1913 (Novello)	Gloucester	Produced at the Gloucester Musical Festival. Dedicated to H.M. Queen Alexandra.
Messe Solonelle, four voices, soli, chorus, and orchestra	Op. 4	1856, pub. 1857	...	The Mass which Liszt praised (see Part I.).
Tantum Ergo, chorus and organ (S.A.T.B., 2 each)	Op. 5	1856, pub. 1862	...	...
Oratorio de Noël, soli, chorus, and string quintet, harp and organ	Op. 12	1858, pub. 1863	Paris	...
Psalm XVIII., Cœli enarrant soli, chorus, and orchestra	Op. 42	1865	...	...
Messe de Requiem, soli, chorus, and orchestra	Op. 54	1878	Paris	Written in eight days for the funeral of M. Libou.

CHORAL WORKS—(Continued).

Title.	No.	Composed and Published.	Début.	Incidents.
Panis Angelicus, tenor solo, Op. string quintet, and organ	Op. ?	... 1898	...	...
Offertoire pour la Toussaint, Op. 4 voices and organ	Op. ?	... 1898	...	
Psalm CL., "Praise Ye the Lord," double chorus, orchestra, and organ	Op. 127	... 1908, pub. 1908 (Shirmer, New York)	...	Written in thanksgiving for the composer's recovery from an illness during his voyage to America.
Laudate Dominum, chorus	Op. 149	... 1918	...	...
Trois Chœurs, for female voices	Op. 151	... 1918	...	...
Les Soldats de Gédéon (Gallet), double chorus for men	Op. 46	...	...	...
Two Choruses (Hugo)	Op. 53	... 1878, pub. 1878	...	
(1) Chanson de Grand-père, two female voices & piano				
(2) Chanson d'Ancêtre, baritone solo, with male chorus, pianoforte and orchestra				
Two Choruses (Saint-Saëns)	Op. 68	... 1882, pub. 1883	...	
(1) Calme des Nuits				
(2) Les Fleurs et les Arbres, 4 mixed voices, pianoforte *ad lib.*				
Two Choruses (T. Saint-Felix)	Op. 71	... 1884, pub. 1884	...	
(1) Les Marins de Kermor				
(2) Les Titans unaccompanied, 4 male voices				

Saint-Saëns has also composed for Church use several settings of motets and hymns :—" Veni Creator "; " Ave Maria "; (5) " Ave Verum "; (3) " O Salutaris "; (6) " Tantum ergo "; (2) " Inviolata "; " Deus Abraham "; " Pie Jesu "; and " Quam dilecta," &c., &c.

LESSER VOCAL WORKS.

Title.	No.	Composed and Published.	Début.	Incidents.
Sérénade d'hiver (Henri Cazalis) 4 male voices	Op. ?	1867, pub. 1868 ...		
Saltarelle (Em. Deschamps) 4 male voices, unaccompanied	Op. 74	1885, pub. 1885 ...		
Les Guerriers, 4 male voices	Op. 84	...		
Madrigal (on the Psyché of Molière), tenor solo and male voices	Op. ?	1897, pub. 1897 ...		
Chants d'Automne, 4 male voices	Op. 113	1899, pub. 1899 ...		
Romance du Soir (J. L. Croze), 4 mixed voices, unaccompanied	Op. ?	1902, pub. 1902 ...		
A la France (J. Combarieu), 4 male or 4 mixed voices unaccompanied	Op. 121	1904, pub. 1904 ...		
Ode d'Horace (Book I., ch. 3), 4 male voices, unaccompanied	Op. ?	1905, pub. 1905 ...		
Le Matin (Lamartine), 4 male voices	Op. 129	1908, pub. 1909 ...		
La Gloire (Auger de Lassus), 4 male voices	Op. 131	1909, pub. 1909 ...		
A Deux (Little Canon for two child's voices)	Op. ?	1909 in a supplement to "Le Revue Musicale" of 15.7. and 1.10.1909 ...		
Two Vocal Quartets (1) Des Pas dans l'allée (2) Trinquons	Op. 141	1914 ...		
Hymne au Travail, 4 male voices	Op. 142	1914 ...		

LESSER VOCAL WORKS—(Continued).

Title.	No.	Composed and Published.	Début.	Incidents.
Ave Maria				
La Cendre Rouge (G. Docquois), Op. 146	Op. 145			
(1) Prélude (2) Ame Triste				
(3) Douceur (4) Silence				
(5) Pâques (6) Jour de pluie				
(7) Amoroso (8) Mai				
(9) Petite Main (10) Reviens				
Tu es Petrus, 4 voices ... Op. 147				
Quam Dilecta, 4 voices, organ Op. 148				
and harp ad lib.				
God Save the King (translated Op. ? ... 1914				
and harmonised)				

203

SONGS (*Accompaniment for Pianoforte, unless otherwise stated*).

Title.		Words by
Guitare (1851 Choudens) ...	...	Victor Hugo
Rêverie (1851) ...	...	Victor Hugo
Le Pas d'Armes du Roi Jean (1852) ...	...	Victor Hugo
La Feuille du Peuplier ...	...	Mme. A. Tastu
L'Attente ...	...	Victor Hugo
La Cloche ...	...	Victor Hugo
Lever de la Lune ...	...	?
Pastorale (Duet) ...	...	Destouches
Le Sommeil des fleurs ...	...	G. de Penmarch
Madonna col Bambino ...	...	
Viens (Duet) ...	...	Victor Hugo
Le Soir descend sur la Colline (Duet) ...	...	
La Mort d'Ophélia ...	...	E. Legouvé

SONGS—(Continued).

Title.	Words by
Souvenances	F. Lemaire
Etoiles du Matin	C. Distel
Extase	Victor Hugo
Soirée en Mer	Victor Hugo
Alla riva del Tebro	
Canzonetta Toscana	
Le Matin	Victor Hugo
L'Enlèvement	Victor Hugo
Clair de Lune	Catulle Mendès
La Coccinelle	Victor Hugo
A Quoi bon Entendre	Victor Hugo (Choudens)
Le chant de ceux qui vont sur la mer ...	Victor Hugo (Choudens)
Tristesse	F. Lemaire
Marquise, vous souvenez vous?	F. Coppée (Choudens)
Maria Lucrezia	F. Legouvé
Mélodies Persanes (Six Songs, Op. 26) ...	Armand Renaud
A Voice by the Cedar Tree	Tennyson (Augener)
Night Song of Preciosa	T. Ginner (Boosey)
Si Vous n'avez rien à me dire	Victor Hugo
Désir de L'Orient	Saint-Saëns
My Land	T. Davis (Boosey)
Dans ton Cœur	Henri Cazalis
Danse Macabre	Henri Cazalis
Vogue, Vogue la galère	Jean Aicard
Dans les coins bleus	Sainte-Beuve
Une flûte invisible	Victor Hugo
Suzette et Suzon	Victor Hugo
Chanson à boire du Vieux Temps	N. Boileau
Présage de la Croix	S. Bordese
Guitares et Mandolines	Saint-Saëns
Amour Viril	G. Boyer

205

SONGS—(Continued).

Title.	Words by
S'il est un charmant gazon (1915)	Victor Hugo
Vive la France (1915)	P. Fournier
Victoire (1918)	P. Fournier
La Française (Chant héroïque de la Grande Guerre) (1915)	N. Zamacois
Ne l'oubliez pas (1914)	
Les Sapins (1917)	
Honneur à l'Amerique	P. Martin

TRANSCRIPTIONS BY SAINT-SAËNS.

Composer.	Work Transcribed.	Transcription for
J. S. Bach	Prélude, Sixth Sonata for violin	Pianoforte (Six, No. 1)
J. S. Bach	Sarabande, violin	Pianoforte (Six, No. 2)
L. Van Beethoven	Ruins of Athens (Chorus of Dervishes)	With pianoforte accomp'nt or orchestra
L. Van Beethoven	String Quartets	Pianoforte (three transcriptions)
L. Van Beethoven	Concerto in G, for pianoforte & orchestra	Pedal point added
L. Van Beethoven	,, for violin and orchestra	Cadenzas added
Hector Berlioz	Damnation de Faust (Easter Hymn)	Pianoforte
Hector Berlioz	Lélio	Pianoforte score (Costallat)
Georges Bizet	Les Pêcheurs de Perles (Scherzo)	Pianoforte (Choudens)
F. Chopin	Sonata in B flat minor	Arranged for two pianofortes
Henri Duparc	Lenore (Poème Symphonique)	Arranged for two pianofortes (Rouart Lerolle)
Jacques Durand	Chansons des Mancroix	Pianoforte
A. Duvernoy	Hellé (Nocturne)	Pianoforte (Enoch)
Gluck	Alceste (opera)	Caprice sur les airs de ballet for pianoforte

TRANSCRIPTIONS BY SAINT-SAËNS—(*Continued*).

Composer.	Work Transcribed.	Transcription for
Gluck	Orphée (opera)	Menuet arranged for pianoforte
Charles Gounod	Faust (opera ; *Kermesse*)	Pianoforte (Choudens)
Charles Gounod	Faust (opera ; Valse)	Pianoforte (Choudens)
Charles Gounod	Gallia	Paraphrase for pianoforte (Novello)
Charles Gounod	Faust (opera ; Kermesse et Valse)	Pianoforte (Choudens)
Charles Gounod	Concert Suite	Arranged for two pianofortes (Leduc)
Haydn	Symphony No. 36 (*Andante*)	Arranged for pianoforte
F. Liszt	Beethoven Cantata	Improvisation for pianoforte (Kahnt, Leipzig)
F. Liszt	Orphée (Poéme Symphonique)	Arranged for pianoforte, violin, et violoncello (Breitkopf and Härtel)
F. Liszt	La Perédiction aux oiseaux (Legend pour piano)	Organ (Rozsavolgzi, Buda-Pesth)
Lwoff	Fantasia on Russian National Anthem (*i.e.*, pre-war)	Pianoforte (Leduc)
J. Massenet	Thais (opera)	Pianoforte paraphrase (Heugel)
F. Mendelssohn-Bartholdy.	Midsummer Night's Dream (Scherzo)	Pianoforte
L. Milan de Valence (16th Century Spanish composer)	Two Fantasias for lute	Pianoforte
W. Mozart	Andante	Pianoforte and violin, or orchestra
Paladilhe	La Mandolinata	Pianoforte paraphrase (Heugel)
Henri Reber	Four Symphonies	Pianoforte duet (Costallat)
R. Schumann	Night Song	Pianoforte or orchestra
R. Wagner	Lohengrin (opera ; Marche religieuse)	Pianoforte, violin, and organ
Paladilhe	La Islena	Pianoforte paraphrase (Heugel)

LITERARY WORKS BY SAINT-SAËNS.

Title.	Date.	Publisher.
Harmonie et Mélodie	1885	C. Lévy
Notes sur les décors de Théâtre dans l'antiquité romaine	1886	Baschet
Rimes familières	1891	C. Lévy
Les Crampes des écrivains (comedy, produced at Algiera)	1892	C. Lévy
Charles Gounod, et le " Don Juan " de Mozart	1893	P. Ollendorff
Problèmes et Mystères	1894	Flammarion
Préface à Hypnotisme, Religion by Dr. Felix Regnault	1897	Schleicher frères
Portraits et Souvenirs	1899	Société d'éditions artistique
Essai sur les lyres et cithares antiques	1902	Didot
Le Roi Apépi (comedy after Cherbuliez, produced at Béziers	1903	C. Lévy
La Art du Théâtre (préface à Les Annales du Théâtre et de la Musique, by E. Stoullig)	1904	P. Ollendorff
Préface to Histoire de la Musique, by Paul Viardot	1905	P. Ollendorff
Préface to Pieces de Clavecin de Rameau	1905	Durand
Préface to Gounod, by J. G. Prod'homme and A. Dandelot	1911	Delagrave
École Buissonière	1913	Pierre Lafitte
Au Courant de la Vie	1914	Dorbon-ainé
Germanophile	1916	Dorbon-ainé
Les Idées de M. Vincent d'Indy	1919	Pierre Lafitte
Musical Memories (being an English translation (E. Giles Rich) of 23 of the 36 essays in " École Buissonière ")	1921	John Murray

Saint-Saëns for many years wrote letters to the leading Parisian musical press :—" Le Revue Musicale "; " Le Monde Musicale "; " Comædia "; " Le Nouvelle Revue."

BIBLIOGRAPHY.

(Unless otherwise stated the following Books are in French.)

Title.	Author.	Date.	Publisher.
Henry VIII.	Ch. Gounod	1883	Imprimerie chaix
Henry VIII., et l'Opéra Française	E. Hippeau	1883	Imp. de Schiller
Profils de Musiciens	Hugues Imbert	1888	Fischbacher
M. Camille Saint-Saëns	Camille Bellaigue	1889	Durand
Ascanio	Ch. Gounod	1890	Durand
Notations Artistiques	Guy Ropartz	1891	Lemerre
Musiciens d'Aujourd'hui (1st volume)	Adolphe Jullien	1892	Lib. de l'Art
" " (2nd volume)	Adolphe Jullien	1894	Lib. de l'Art
Masters of French Music	Arthur Bervey (English)...	1894	Osgood, McIlvaine
Franz Liszt, " Letters " Collected and edited by La Mara and translated by Constance Bache (English)		1894	H. Grevel & Co.
Mémoires d'un artiste	Ch. Gounod	1896	C. Lévy
Une Partition méconnue, Proserpine	Etienne Destranges	1895	Fischbacher
Musique	Adolphe Jullien	1896	Fischbacher
La Musique Française moderne	Georges Servières	1897	Havard
Camille Saint-Saëns	Otto Neitzel (German)	1899	Harmonie (Berlin)
Camille Saint-Saëns and Déjanire	Emile Baumann	1900	Durand
Musiques d'Hier et de Demain	Alfred Bruneau	1900	Fasquelle
Mastersingers	Filson Young (English)...	1901	W. Reeves
La Musique Française	Alfred Bruneau	1901	Fasquelle
From Greig to Brahms	Dan Gregory Mason (English)	1901	Outlook Co. (New York)
Musiques de Russie et Musiciens de France	Alfred Bruneau	1903	Fasquelle
French Music in the 19th Century	Arthur Hervey (English).	1903	Grant Richards
Groves' Dictionary of Musicians	J. A. Fuller-Maitland Editor (English)	1904	Macmillan

BIBLIOGRAPHY—(*Continued*).

Title.	Author.	Date	Publisher.
Les Grandes Formes de la Musique, L'œuvre ... de C. Saint-Saëns	... Emile Baumann	... 1905 ...	P. Ollendorff
Consonnances et Dissonances	... Etienne Destranges	... 1906 ...	Fischbacher
Samson et Dalila	... Etienne Destranges	...	Durand
Programme Music in the last four centuries ...	Frederick Niecks, Mus. Doc. (English)	... 1906 ...	Novello
Musiciens d'Aujourd'hui	... Romain Rolland	... 1908 ...	Hachette
Cours de Composition Musicale	... Vincent d'Indy	... 1909 ...	Durand
Musiciens d'Hier et d'Aujourd'hui	... Adolphe Jullien	... 1910 ...	Fischbacher
Musiciens Française d'Aujourd'hui	... Octave Séré	... 1911 ...	Mercure de France
The History of the Philharmonic Society of London	... Myles Birket Foster (English)	... 1912 ...	John Lane
C. Saint-Saëns	... Jean Bonnerot	... 1914 ...	Durand
Memories of a Musician	... W. Ganz (English)	... 1913 ...	John Murray
Reminiscences, Impressions and Anecdotes ...	Francesco Berger (English)	...	Samson, Low, Marston & Co.
Camille Saint-Saëns	... Jean Montargis	... 1919 ...	La Renaissance du Livre
Saint-Saëns	... Arthur Hervey (English)...	... 1921 ...	John Lane